FISHING SECRETS

FISHING SECRETS

101 WAYS TO IMPROVE YOUR FISHING

JEROME KNAP

CROWN PUBLISHERS INC.
NEW YORK

 Copyright © 1977 PAGURIAN PRESS LIMITED
Suite 1106, 335 Bay Street, Toronto, Canada

A Christopher Ondaatje publication.
Copyright under the Berne Convention. All rights reserved. No part of this book may be reproduced in any form without the permission of the publishers.

Library of Congress Cataloging in Publication Data

Knap, Jerome J.
  Fishing secrets.

1. Fishing.   I. Title.
SH441.K57 1978   799.1   77-15940
ISBN 0-517-53309-X

Printed and bound in the United States

Contents

Introduction 9

1. Take a Kid Out Fishing 11
2. Practice Makes Fishermen 12
3. Water Temperature — The Secret of Successful Fishing 14
4. Casting a Fly Is Easy 17
5. How to False Cast and Get the Line Out 22
6. How to Read a Stream 25
7. Tactics for Small Streams 27
8. Stream-Seasoned Smallmouths Need Trout Tactics 29
9. Stream Fishing with Spinners 30
10. Mini-System Fishing Secrets 31
11. Proper Drag — Your Best Friend in Fighting Big Fish 34
12. Time and Fishing 37
13. Anyone Can Catch Big Fish 39
14. Outfitting Your Tackle Box 42
15. A Tool for the Tackle Box 43
16. Hone Your Hooks 44
17. It's All in the Line 45
18. It's Time We Changed Knots 46
19. The Uni-Knot — An Easy Knot for All Fishing 49
20. For Trout — Flyfish the Edges 55
21. The Myth of the Long Cast 58
22. Nymph + Dry Fly = Trout! 60
23. Nymphs and Streamers Are Trout Favorites 61
24. Drifting Them Deep 64
25. Weighted Flies for Fast Water 66
26. Get to Know the Caddis 66
27. Caddis Techniques 69
28. The Latex Caddis 70
29. Catching Trophy Bass 72

30. Ripping for Bass   74
31. Bass Bugging on Lakes or Ponds   77
32. More Bass-Bugging Techniques   79
33. Try the Deer-Hair Frog   81
34. Bucktails for Bass   82
35. Jigs Are Hard to Beat   83
36. How to Catch More Fish on Jigs   86
37. Windy Weather Lures   87
38. Rigs for Bluegills   88
39. Secrets of Successful Crappie Fishing   89
40. Give Carp a Try   93
41. Separating the Pike-Perches   97
42. For Summer Walleyes, Keep Moving Deep and Slow   98
43. For Walleyes Try Some Moonshine   100
44. Don't Neglect Gravel Bars   101
45. Separating the Pikes   101
46. Fishing for Old Sharptooth   102
47. Psyching a Pike   105
48. How to Fish Weedbeds   107
49. To Catch a Muskie   108
50. Separating the Salmonids   110
51. Steelheading Is a Matter of Feel   111
52. Lure-Drifting for River Rainbows   113
53. Drift Rig for Bottom Steelheads   115
54. Nymph Fishing the Easy Way   115
55. Fishing Dry Flies   116
56. The Marabou Magic   117
57. Unbeatable Bass Bait   120
58. Rigging the Plastic Worm   124
59. The Knot for Plastic Worms   126
60. Curing the Sliding Worm Problem   128
61. Inside Dope on Fishing   128
62. A Real Worm Turns   129
63. Cool Tips for Storing Nightcrawlers   130
64. Raise Your Own Worms   132
65. Tempt Walleyes with Leeches   134
66. Frogs Rarely Fail   135

67. Keeping Hooked Bait Alive   136
68. The Best Bait for Ice Fishing   136
69. Deadly Steelhead Bait   137
70. The Deadly Bait   139
71. Quiet! Fish Can Hear   140
72. Careful! Fish Can Smell   141
73. Fish by the Barometer   143
74. Sonar: A Must for the Sophisticated Fisherman   145
75. The Downrigger for Deep-Dwelling Fish   147
76. Formula for Successful Trolling   148
77. Try the Countdown for Different Water Levels   152
78. Deep-Running Rigs   153
79. How to Ice-Fish with Artificials   153
80. How Not to Do the Twist   155
81. Getting Out the Twist   156
82. Using Marked Line   156
83. Be a Tippet Switcher   157
84. How to Fly Fish with a Spinning Rod   160
85. Bunker Dunking for Big Stripers   161
86. A Trick for Minnow Chasing White Bass   163
87. When the Bass Aren't Biting   164
88. Spinnerbait Basics for More Bass   165
89. Tandem Hooks for Small Spinnerbaits   167
90. Fish the Windward Shore   168
91. Never Say Die   169
92. The Next Fish You Catch May Be a Record Fish   170
93. Give the Taxidermist a Break   172
94. Dry Hands Are Best   173
95. Artificial Respiration for Fish   174
96. How to Remove an Imbedded Hook   176
97. Cleaning Panfish   178
98. How to Skin a Fish   179
99. How to Fillet a Fish   179
100. How to Pickle Fish   182
101. How to Cook a Shore Lunch   184

Acknowledgments   197

Introduction

The chatter of a brook, the roar of a swift river, and the soft thud of waves lapping at a rocky shoreline may well be swan songs. Greed has turned many of our streams into open sewers and our lakes into cesspools. Skull and crossbones and "no swimming" signs, signs advising anglers to "fish for fun" because the fish are dangerous to eat — these are chilling examples of what we are doing to our waters.

If you want to enjoy fishing for a long time to come, if you want your children and your children's children to enjoy it, join the war against pollution. How? First, join a local sportsman's and anti-pollution association. Then, join national organizations such as the National Wildlife Federation and the Izaak Walton League. Let your voice be heard.

Fight pollution on a personal level. Pack up your garbage. Don't litter streams and lakeshores with your lunch wrappers, pop cans, or the viscera of the fish you have cleaned. If you see anyone doing this, don't shut your eyes to it. Tell him to clean up his mess or you will testify in a court of law against him.

Pollution can be prevented.

In summer when the water temperature rises, trout frequently move close to where water tumbles over rocks. Why? As water temperature rises, oxygen decreases. But where you see white water tumbling over rocks, there's bound to be plenty of oxygen.

TIP NO. 1

Take a Kid Out Fishing

One of the most memorable pictures in a family album is usually a snapshot of a father and son fishing. It represents a moment of solitude when their thoughts are united by a common interest.

Fishing is a sport everyone can enjoy. Age and sex are no barriers, and the experiences that are shared between parents and children on such solitary excursions are important milestones in their relationship to each other.

Teaching a child to fish requires self-discipline. Your initial fishing trip should be short: spend a few hours letting the child fish on his own terms. Do not coach or be too helpful. Let mistakes happen. Above all, make the first day enjoyable. After fishing, analyze the mistakes that were made. Explain why the fish that was hooked came off or how the reel developed the bird's nest tangled line. Be patient.

Learning experiences acquired in the course of several fishing excursions have more meaning and last longer than trying to teach everything on the first outing.

One thing you can be certain of — if a child gets hooked on fishing, and has opportunities to fish, he won't have much time to run with a gang, pop pills, or worse.

To catch trout in small streams, you must develop some unorthodox techniques, such as wading downstream to beat the brush.

TIP NO. 2

Practice Makes Fishermen

It is curious but true, that fishermen won't practice. Practice catching fish? No, practice accurate casting, the touchstone to catching fish. Golfers practice. Bowlers practice. Shotgunners practice. Archers practice. Even deer hunters "zero in" their rifles.

If a golfer, an *amateur* golfer, has a Sunday tournament, he'll be on the driving range Wednesday slugging out a bucket of balls. Before tee-off he'll stroke his way around the practice green. In addition, he'll take a mulligan off the first tee!

But the fisherman won't practice. He just goes. Who knows how many fish he misses through inaccurately placed casts or how much fishing time he loses through backlashes or kinky spinning line too "set" to his reel.

Well, he should practice. The fisherman who lays a plug an inch from a snag on his first cast fills his stringer; his erratic companion, two feet off target, goes fishless. Sometimes (most times) a bass won't move that far for a feed.

The lure with a worm trailer which seems to "drift" into the water without a sound like a water snake draws an immediate response. The heavy, loud cast is ignored. It can't fool a foxy bass or a savvy muskie or even a hungry pike.

What kind of practice? The answer is backyard casting at targets. Nail some paper plates to the ground at odd intervals. Put one target under the arms of a birch or a eucalyptus or a maple. Buy practice plugs of the proper weight at the tackle store.

Keep the elbow close and fix that "clock" casting chart in your mind. Point the target. Pull back smartly to 1 o'clock. Let

Practice makes fishermen.

go at 11. Try overhead casts first, then from the side and underhand.

Check the reel. Is it working smoothly? Does the bale remain down during the cast as it is supposed to, or does it snap back early, an embarrassment later on?

Is the line smooth to the touch or is it nicked? Is it kinky? Should it be replaced? Is it up to reel capacity which aids the cast? Now is the time for remedial action — not while at the fishing hole when you'd much rather fish.

Shoot at the targets from various distances. Use different-weight practice plugs. Work on style. Keep your elbow close. Be aware of your backcast; do not endanger a companion. Whatever the routine, develop steady practice habits. Warm up before that fishing trip. The payoff is more fish on the stringer — through practice.

TIP NO. 3

Water Temperature — The Secret of Successful Fishing

For years commercial fishermen, whose livelihood depends on catching fish, have used electronic thermometers to locate their quarry. Although their equipment is too bulky and expensive for the sport fisherman, the same principle has been applied to inexpensive yet effective temperature readers, which are now available.

A five-pound bass like this one from Lake of the Woods is a trophy fish in the northern states and Canada. But it would have to weigh twice that to attract much attention in Florida. Why? Southern bass have a longer growing season.

Water temperature is important in your search for fish. Fish are cold-blooded and their body temperatures match that of the surrounding water. Most fish are sensitive to temperature changes as slight as three degrees; they usually prefer to remain in a narrow temperature band.

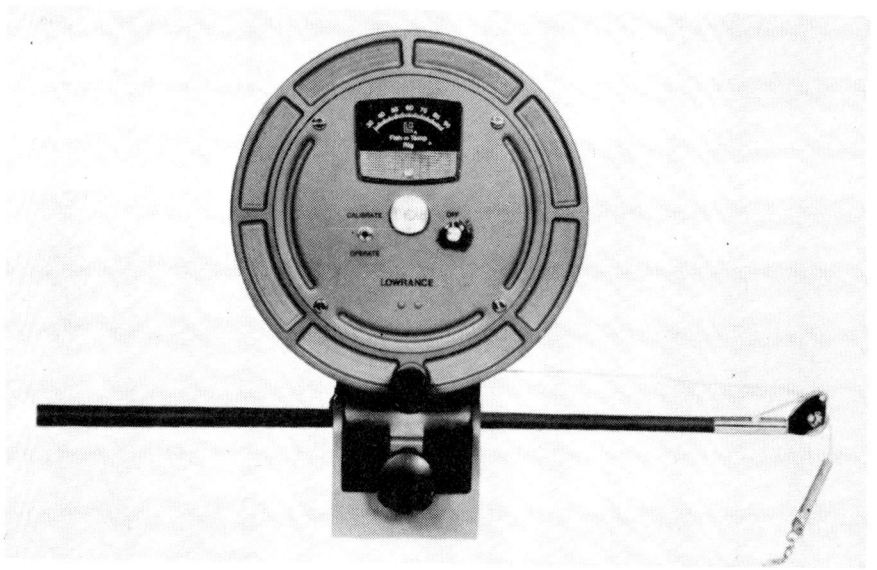

One of the newest instruments for temperature fishing is the LTG 200 Fish-n-Temp. It is both a downrigger and an electronic thermometer.

Water temperatures directly affect their digestive and metabolic rate. The lower the water temperature, the lower the digestive rate. As the water becomes warmer, a fish's digestive and metabolic rates increase, causing it to feed more. When water becomes either too hot or too cold, fish tend to become inactive and feed listlessly if at all. Find fish in their maximum comfort zone, however, and you'll find them ready for action. Of course there are seasonal periods when fish inhabit and feed in unusually cold or warm water. Ice fishermen get good catches, but the fish are sometimes sluggish.

In the early spring when the water is cool, fish often feed wildly; it's probably the warming trend of the water rather than the actual temperature that gets them going.

With an electronic fishing thermometer, you can make a series of readings at depths up to one hundred feet without having to raise or lower the apparatus. You simply lower the sensory element or thermistor on a cord and instantly read the temperature on a dial held in your hand. As the element moves vertically through the water, changes in water temperature are indicated on the meter. Unlike a mercury thermometer, there is no waiting to get a reading — you use the electronic thermometer to find a preferred temperature relative to the depth, and so make the most of your time on the water by fishing only in productive areas.

TIP NO. 4

Casting a Fly Is Easy

The mechanics of fly casting are simple. The line is thrown back through the air by the movement of the rod; the instant it straightens out behind the caster's shoulder, the rod is brought forward, and the line is thrown forward through the air. The key is to let the line straighten out behind you before driving the rod forward. You actually cast the line; the fly goes along for the ride.

The best place to begin is on smooth, cut grass. You need an open space about eighty feet long. Stand in the middle of it. Lay the assembled outfit flat on the grass, with the reel handle up; walk away from it with the fly until you have pulled about thirty feet of line out of the guides.

Hold the rod pointed down the line toward the fly. Your grasp on the grip should be firm but not tight. Most good casters extend the thumb toward the tip on top of the grip — the side opposite the reel. Guides and reel should be down. Hold the line firmly in your left hand between the reel and the first guide.

Your feet should be comfortably apart, both quartering to the right. In other words, instead of facing squarely toward the line stretched out on the grass, which is the direction in which you're going to cast, your feet should be at about forty-five degrees from it. This, of course, only applies if you're right-handed. Anyone who is left-handed reverses the angle. You are about to make a back cast, and the reason for standing in this position is so that you can watch the line over your right shoulder.

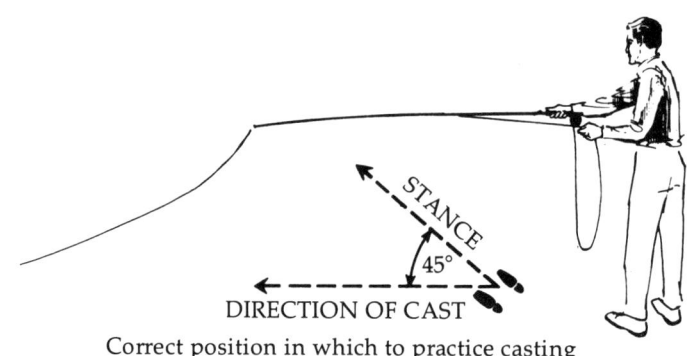

Correct position in which to practice casting

You are standing angled to the right, with your right elbow about three inches in front of your belly; forearm and rod pointed straight down the line. Your wrist will necessarily be bent down. It will remain in this position until the back cast is nearly made. Your left hand, holding the line, should be out toward the rod grip.

The back cast is made with the elbow and shoulder; the wrist remains locked in the position previously described. Start the line coming toward you on the grass by raising the elbow to lift the rod. The movement is up and back, accelerating rapidly. Hold the line firmly with your left hand; don't let any of it slip through the guides. As the rod approaches the vertical, pull the line down sharply about a foot.

In all casting directions, the position of the rod is generally referred to in relation to a clock dial, with the rod corresponding to the hour hand. Hence, 9 o'clock would be with your rod straight out from you, 3 o'clock would be with your rod straight behind you, and 12 o'clock would be with your rod vertical.

By the time the rod reaches the 11 o'clock position, the line will be coming toward you in the air. Bring the shoulder into play and move the entire rod back about eighteen inches, at the same time pivoting the elbow until the rod is vertical; stop dead. The stop is accomplished by tensing your forearm, wrist and hand; then relaxing immediately.

The whole movement is brisk and continuous. Don't simply sweep the rod through the air; make it bend. Finally permit the rod to tip back to one o'clock by bending the wrist. This doesn't contribute to the back cast, however, but puts the rod into position to start the forward cast.

If you have done everything properly, the line will fairly hiss out behind, passing above the rod tip, and straighten. It will be parallel to the ground and as high above it as the rod tip at the conclusion of the backward movement. Watch it over your shoulder.

If the line doesn't straighten, let it fall to the grass, turn around, back away to pull out whatever slack may be present, then try again. The sole purpose of the back cast is to put the line into position to receive the force of the forward cast. Without a good back cast a good forward cast is impossible.

Now, let's assume that either on the first or second attempt, the line goes out straight and true. While the loop or "U" is turning over, raise your left hand, still clutching the line tightly, about a foot. This line will be pulled out through the guides, ready for the forward cast.

When you've made a good back cast with the line out straight behind and tugging against the rod, you're ready to make the forward cast. Your right hand will be a few inches higher than your shoulder and somewhat behind it. Your left hand, holding the line, will be up toward the right shoulder.

Without changing the angle of your wrist, bring the entire rod forward, still in its one o'clock position. This is a full-arm movement by shoulder and elbow, made somewhat as though you were pushing a weight along a shoulder-high table. Accelerate briskly. Keep the reel above your shoulder. Don't lower it.

As your arm approaches the straight-out-in-front position, tip the rod forward to 11 o'clock by rotating your wrist and again come to a dead stop by tensing your arm muscles, then immediately relaxing them. Learning to stop dead at the end of the back and forward casts is the most important part of fly casting. The stop forces the tip over extremely fast, increasing the speed of the line. Simultaneously, lower your left hand about a foot, while it is still holding the line.

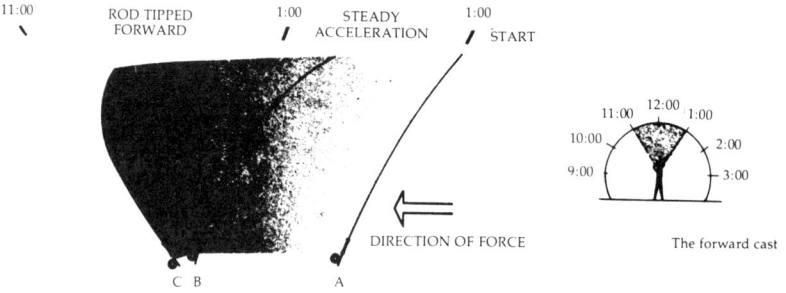

The forward cast

Again, the entire rod arm makes a brisk, pushing movement with the turn of the wrist coming at its conclusion. The rod stays in the same vertical plane, both back and ahead.

Let the line straighten, then fall to the grass, lowering the rod and arm as it does. If the line fails to straighten, you've probably waved the rod, rather than pushed it smartly. If the leader and fly whip around and double back, you've used more force than necessary — unusual for beginners; most act as though the rod would break if they bent it.

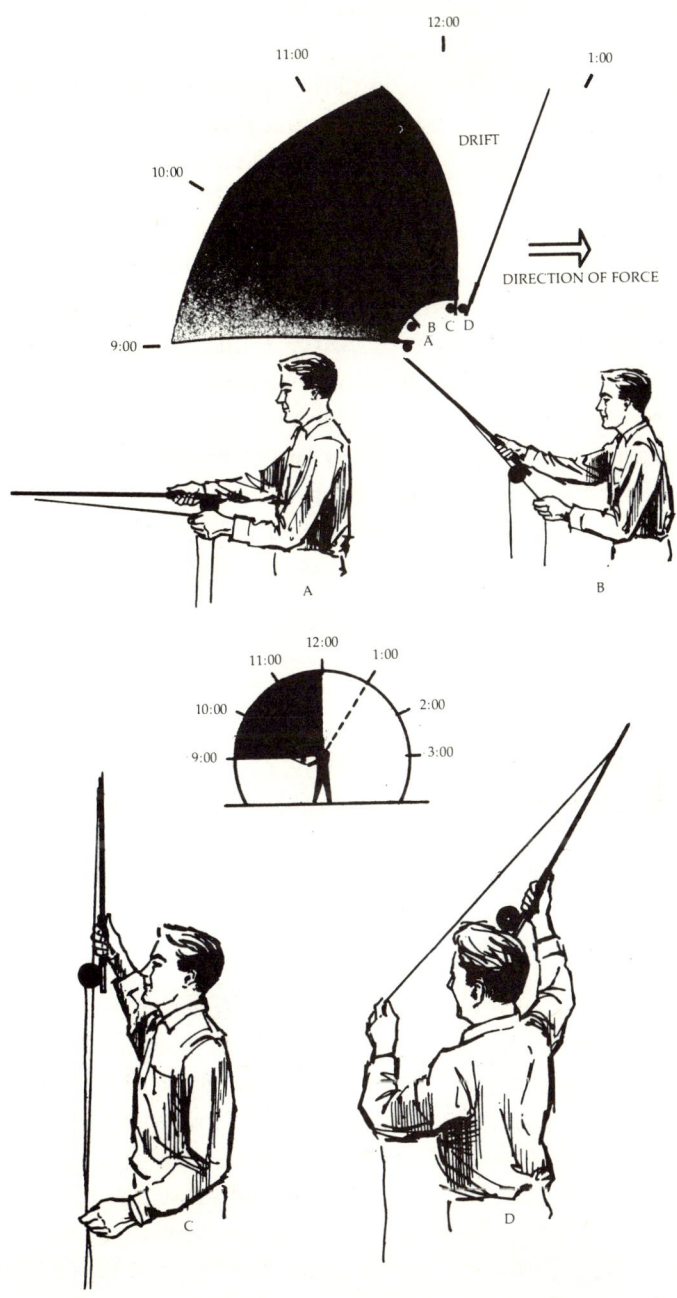

After practicing the forward cast a few minutes (practicing more than a few minutes at a time does no good) look at your leader. It probably will have from one to a dozen knots in it. These are called wind knots, but the wind has nothing to do with them. They're caused by tipping the rod ahead first, then pushing it. Move the entire rod at the start of the cast; tip it ahead with a wrist movement last.

At this point, don't attempt to cast farther. Practice, resting occasionally, until you can make both the back cast and the forward cast perfectly. Remember — the line must straighten behind in the back cast before you can make a good forward cast. This is why you stand where you can watch it. There must always be a pause while the loop unfolds and the rod drifts back. At first you'll have to watch to tell how long to give it. Later, this timing will become completely automatic. You won't even have to think about it, much less watch. And, of course, with the same power, it takes the same length of line just as long to straighten in the back cast as it does in the forward cast.

TIP NO. 5

How to False Cast and Get the Line Out

When you have grasped the mechanics of fly casting, you are ready to work on your false cast and learn how to get more line out.

In false casting, the fly does not touch the water (or, in this case, the grass). False casting is used to work out more line, to change direction, or to whip the water out of a dry fly so that it will float.

Make the first back and forward casts as described, but when the forward cast straightens out, don't let it fall to the grass. Instead, start the back cast immediately. You will find this is actually easier than starting the back cast from the grass.

Following a false cast, with the line higher out in front, the back cast is more a horizontal movement. Normally angled only slightly upward, it is done much the same as the forward cast, except in the opposite direction.

Don't let the rod drift down farther than 10 o'clock on the forward cast. Start the line back as soon as it is straight. Watch your back cast until you can make it straighten properly every time and until timing the pause for it to do so becomes automatic.

The beginner's most common fault, next to waving his rod rather than accelerating it briskly, is to let line slip out through the guides at the start of both the back cast and the forward cast. Guard against this. If you hold the line tightly in your left hand and pull a little each time, this will not happen.

The line speed that makes casting possible comes from energy supplied by the caster through the rod. If you permit the line to slip out through the guides while the rod moves, no energy is transmitted to the line; consequently, the line won't go anywhere.

Right now the devil is rearing his ugly head. You may not recognize him because he's a sly rascal, but he's already whispering in your ear. He's saying, "Let out a little more line. Let's see if you can cast a little farther." Don't do it! In fly casting, as in any other sport requiring muscular coordination, form is everything. If you achieve correct form first, long casts will come with virtually no effort. If you don't learn correct form, you will never be able to make long casts.

Instead of attempting to cast farther, continue practicing with thirty feet of line past the rod tip. Actually, this thirty feet plus an eight-foot rod and a seven-and-a-half-foot leader add up to more than forty-five feet. You'll seldom want to cast a dry fly past forty-five feet when you're fishing for trout, and you'll never really need to cast farther for panfish. So you see, you're already casting far enough to catch fish, and perfect control at this distance will do you far more good than straining to cast twice as far.

About this time you will probably discover that your back cast is hitting the ground behind. This is caused by continuing the application of power too far back. You may actually be stopping your rod at 3 o'clock, even though you intend to stop it at 12 o'clock. Have someone watch to check on this. Remember, if you keep your wrist stiff you will do it right.

Working Out Line

You started casting by pulling line out along the grass from the rod tip. Now that you can false cast, you're ready to forget this bother. Put the rod tip on the ground and pull six or eight feet of line from the tip. Pick up the rod and pull a yard of line off the reel with the left hand. Raise the rod quickly as though starting a back cast and this line will slip out through the guides.

You now have enough line out to start false casting. Less line of course will require less power, but again the natural tendency for the beginner is to use too little rather than too much. Strip another yard or so of line from the reel, but hold it firmly while you make a back cast. On the forward cast, instantly after the application of power, let the line go. It will shoot out through the guides.

Immediately strip another yard of line from the reel while making the back cast and release it on the next forward cast. Repeat this process until you have the required thirty feet past the rod tip. Actually, once you become proficient, you can feed line on both back and forward casts and get it out to fishing distance very quickly.

What to practice with thirty feet of line? First, simply false cast, resting every few minutes until you're making every back cast and forward cast perfectly. Let an occasional forward cast fall to the grass as though you were actually fishing.

Next, try for accuracy. Put a target on the grass and see how close you can come to dropping your fly on it. Try not to watch your back cast to see if you've memorized the length of pause needed for it to straighten.

At this stage, you'll undoubtedly get some sharp cracks, like snapping a whip, and you may actually pop your fly off — caused by starting the forward cast too soon. Give the back cast a little more time to straighten out.

Before long the tackle will no longer feel strange. You won't have to think about every aspect of every cast, and both hands will be doing their part automatically and correctly.

TIP NO. 6

How to Read a Stream

Trout fishing is more than catching fish; the lore and lure of angling is understanding the habits and habitat of the quarry, an awareness of where trout are going to be in a stream and why. Almost everyone knows that trout face into the current; that is, upstream, because that is the direction from which their food comes.

Basically, trout must have a source of food, cover, and a good supply of oxygen, coupled with favorable water temperatures. Knowing this you can start to think like a trout. Food is usually swept downstream by the current, so the fish must station itself in a position where it can watch the flow of water. But it takes a great deal of energy for a trout to hold its position in the main stream. It will usually look for spots where the current is broken by a natural obstacle such as a log or a rock, so that it can stay out of the current but be close enough to dart out for a choice morsel.

The fish may also choose to rest on the fringes of the current — under a cut in the bank, or at the tail of a pool where a riffle pours into slightly deeper water. The trick is to be able to present a fly or lure so that it sweeps by the trout's lie naturally. It must look like any other insect or minnow working downstream.

Trout generally lie close to the bottom where the current is slightly diminished, but they look upward for their food. One flick of the tail and a brookie or rainbow is on the trail of its next meal.

Another factor worth considering is the oxygen content of the water. This is often coupled with temperature since, as water temperature rises, oxygen is depleted. As the flowing water tumbles over rocks or passages through riffles, air bubbles are formed. The white water you see is air mixed with water. When necessary trout move into this habitat for extra oxygen.

When trout are searching for food, they'll often move into the head of a pool. The reason is obvious. Most pools are fed by a current and food is concentrated in a narrow band. Once the meal reaches the deep pool, it is harder to find, and that's also the reason why fish concentrate at the tail end of the pool.

It takes a little practice but before long you can actually read the movement of water in a stream and have a fair idea of where the fish are going to be. Then it's a question of approaching carefully, usually from below the fish, and making a presentation that will sweep by the lie. If you've heard veteran anglers tell you to cast across and up current, what they are telling you is to place your bait where it will follow a natural route. And by working upstream, the fish are less apt to see you.

Fly fishermen and dry fly advocates in particular are faced with another problem called drag. The fly should come downstream at the same rate as the current, but the fly line will start to belly, and when the current catches it, the fly is pulled downstream in an arc. To compensate, fly fishermen use a technique known as mending the line, in which they throw a loop of line upstream via a roll-type cast while the fly is still moving downstream.

The next time you work a stream, take a moment to study the water carefully. Look for currents and eddies, deeper pools with shallow heads and tails, natural obstructions that divide the current, and riffles that produce oxygen. Then think in terms of cover for a trout. Where would a trout be if it wanted to feed yet remain hidden? When you have decided, place your fly, lure, or bait in such a position that it will pass close to this line, carried by the current. If a fish is there and feeding, your chances of a strike are good.

TIP NO. 7

Tactics for Small Streams

Some of the best trout fishing is in small brooks — the smaller the better. Small streams never get the recognition, the name and hence the fishing pressure of larger streams; frequently they are completely overlooked. No one seems to realize they have trout and, even when it is known they do, are not fished much because a small stream overgrown with willows, alders, or brambles cannot be successfully fished with conventional techniques. For small streams you need special savvy.

Small streams rarely have much of a spring run-off, so they seldom get murky and muddy. Their narrow widths are amply shaded from the sun by brush. Frequently they are spring fed. These conditions create stable water — clear and cool all season. Trout behave normally and are not difficult to find.

But to catch them unorthodox techniques are needed. The only way to beat the brush is to wade — downstream. Yes, downstream! Wading upstream is fine for big streams where you are free to move about and have plenty of room for casting, but because brush and the width of the small stream are confining, casting into holes, undercut banks and under submerged logs — the usual trout haunts — is almost impossible. By moving downstream, you are always above the trout haunts and all it takes to get your bait to them is to let it drift.

Wading downstream can raise mud clouds that spook fish. It is important that you wade as much as possible on firm footing which has little debris, but disturbing the bottom a little is actually a help. It dislodges nymphs and other trout food.

When it comes to tackle for small streams, there are two choices — an ultra-light spinning outfit or a light seven-foot fly rod. The spinning outfit is preferable in really tight situations: the rod's short length gives you plenty of room to fight a fish. The fly rod is best where you need to be right on a snag-ringed target. You don't cast with the rod; just strip off a few feet of the leader and use the rod like a boy's cane pole. The fly rod's sensitivity will alert you the instant you get a bite or hit a snag.

Small streams are generally rich in food — nymphs, small crawfish, tiny minnows, plus hosts of terrestrial creatures such as grasshoppers, crickets and earthworms. All are good baits, whether artificial or the real thing. I prefer artificial nymphs and small, live, red worms.

When using worms, I like a large hook, as large as No. 4. The trout in small streams are unsophisticated. They continue to swallow even when biting on a steel hook. Using fairly large hooks ensures that tiny trout, too small to keep, won't get the hooks down their gullets and kill themselves. In fact, you won't even hook the little fish.

TIP NO. 8

Stream-Seasoned Smallmouths Need Trout Tactics

Small eastern streams, even those carrying plenty of bass, seldom yield a super-sized smallmouth. In addition, during the summer months these streams run low and clear and the resident bass become as lure-shy and sly as stream-seasoned trout.

The upshot is that small streams, even the best, get little fishing pressure during the warm months. But the very reasons that turn most fishermen away are fine selling points for a light tackle angler looking for a challenge.

The tackle and tactics best suited for these streams are much the same as used on stream-wise trout. Lightweight tackle is the secret — a spinning rod built to handle two to four-pound test line and small lures or a fly rod that can throw a #5 or #6 weight line. In either case, a soft action is in order; it'll do the job without popping light lines and leaders.

The minnow-like Rapala and Rebel plugs in the small two-inch size are good choices for lures. Any midget plug that floats at rest but dives and darts on the retrieve is also worth a try — the action needed in exploring shallow streams for smallmouth bass.

Spinners such as the Mepps or C.P. Swing in the #0 or #1 sizes, with or without squirrel-tail skirts, take their share of bass too, but tend to get caught on the stream bottom. Better yet are small lead-headed marabou jigs, $1/8$ to $1/16$ ounce in weight. These, too, will catch, but not as often since they're light and don't sink as rapidly. They're a fine all-round smallmouth lure.

Poppers, marabou streamers, muddler minnows and fur-bodied nymphs are good bets for the small water flyrodder; hook sizes from #8's to #6's and leaders tapered to 4X fit the bill for most little streams.

In this kind of fishing the approach is as important as equipment. No matter what your usual preference, upstream fishing works best when the water is low and clear. Chances are a smallmouth will be looking upstream and he's less likely to spot your approach and any debris dislodged drifts away from the action.

Keep low. Be sneaky. Avoid fast movements or flashy clothing and tackle that will alarm already spooky bass. Don't make waves; they broadcast your presence and send bass scurrying for cover.

Polaroid glasses will cut surface glare and help you spot where the bass are. Sometimes they'll be right at the lip of a pool, sometimes in quiet pockets to the side of the main current. When the water is low your best chance of taking a bass is on your first cast. It's downhill from then on, unless you rest the pool for ten or fifteen minutes.

TIP NO. 9

Stream Fishing with Spinners

Spinners are best fished upstream across the current. Facing across the current to the opposite bank, cast upstream at about 10 o'clock and reel and work the lure toward you. The spinner fished this way gets a double action — by being tumbled by the current and by being propelled forward by the reeling. Fish will most often strike the spinner as it reaches the end of its downward swing by the current and starts to come directly toward you.

At first fish your spinner as slowly as possible, but don't be afraid to vary the speed with successive casts. You should be able to tell by the feel if the blade is right. The depth of the spinner can be easily controlled by raising or lowering the rod tip, as well as by the speed of your retrieve. Don't be afraid of snags. If you have a sensitive hand, you will feel the revolving blade hit a rock before the hooks do. Raise the rod tip fast and you will avoid most snags.

TIP NO. 10

Mini-System Fishing Secrets

Good equipment is important in all sportfishing. It is twice as important in mini-system fishing. The smaller the reel and the lighter the line, the more quickly your equipment deteriorates.

Choose reels with a great deal of care. First, buy only those that have ball bearing races. Ascertain that the drag is smooth. Select a reel that can be adjusted evenly and quickly. Make sure that the tolerances are close enough to prevent line from getting behind the spool. (The new skirted, open-face reel has solved this major problem for fishermen.)

When selecting a rod, keep in mind that you are going to be casting lures weighing from 1/16 ounce to 3/16 ounce, or at the most, 1/4 ounce; therefore, you must be able to feel an 1/8 ounce weight when casting. Check the guides — you must have as little resistance as possible. I prefer the new ceramic guides as they are very smooth. Be sure the rod has enough guides to avoid line-slapping.

I cannot say enough about the importance of a premium quality line for mini-system fishing. Almost every fish caught with this type of equipment places a tremendous strain on your line. Anything other than the very best will cost you lost fish and lost lures.

Successful techniques for artificial lure fishing with the mini-system equipment do not vary a great deal from techniques used with standard size equipment — they are simply more refined because of the delicate equipment.

To become a successful fisherman, accuracy in casting is an absolute must. Casting to open water usually does not produce fish, and casting inaccurately into obstructions and weed beds results in hang-ups, spooked fish and lost lures.

Proper presentation of lures is the second most important skill to master. Present your lure with a lifelike action. Surface lures should drop lightly into the shadows of obstructions and rocks. Allow them to rest until all the ripples have disappeared; then twitch very lightly. Repeat this action two or three times depending on the size of the obstruction or the length of the shadow. Fish the lure all the way back to the boat.

Smaller lures do not spook fish nearly as much, consequently they will follow the lure a greater distance. Medium-running lures should be swimming, darting, stopping and starting all the way back to the boat. Cast beyond good cover and make sure the lure is working for you at the right spot. Spinner baits and spinners, like medium-running lures, should be working as they pass protective cover or drop into weed-bed pockets when fish are seeking food. Deep-running lures should be vibrating, bouncing off the bottom, swimming from obstruction to obstruction all the way back to the boat. I have found that fish can't resist a crank bait when it bounces off an obstruction or off the bottom, becoming disoriented on its retrieve.

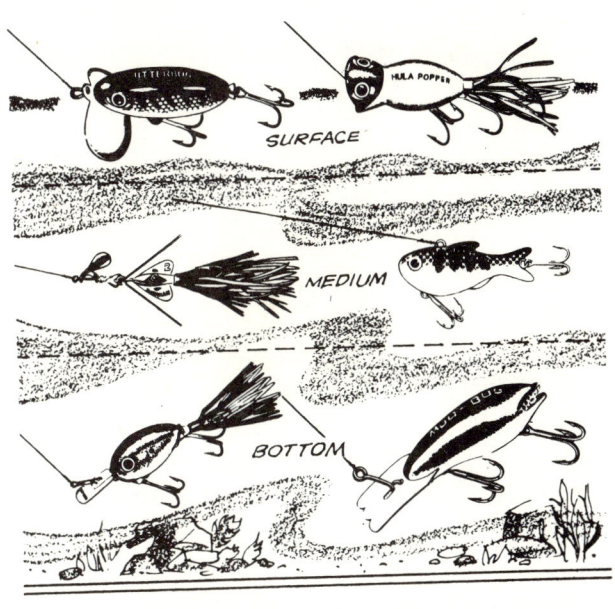
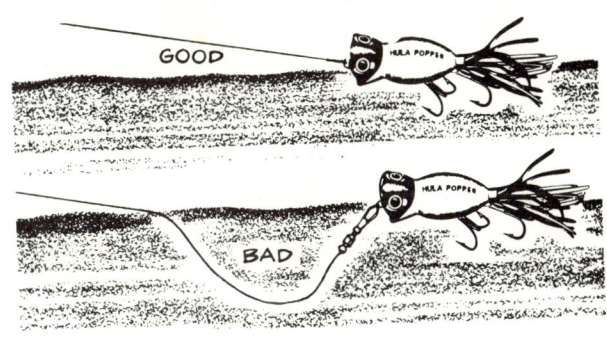
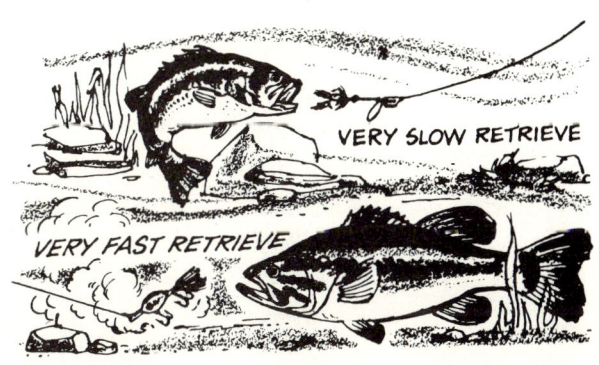

All sport fishermen attempting to catch a trophy fish with light equipment quickly learn the absolute necessity for proper knots. I like to use a palomar knot when tying directly to the lure (I do not use a snap or snap swivel with these small lures). Another of my favorite knots is the double — or spider hitch — or, as it is referred to in salt water fishing, the "Bimini." The only way to learn how to tie good, foolproof knots is to practice. Tie them over and over again until you become so familiar with them that they become automatic.

A tremendous advantage of mini-system fishing is that one can get a great deal of excitement and fun out of fishing close to home. The combination of smaller lures and a quiet approach enhance one's chances of catching fish in heavily fished waters. One can fish farm ponds, strip pits, and even some of the urban reservoirs where lures and heavier equipment are unsuccessful.

But the very feature that makes mini-system fishing exciting also causes the most problems. A combination of light line, small reels and short rods creates a situation that requires skill and patience.

TIP NO. 11

Proper Drag — Your Best Friend in Fighting Big Fish

Most fishermen, even after their lines have been snapped by a trophy-sized fish, rarely try to determine why. There are a number of reasons why a line snaps, but the most common is a poorly set drag.

The principle of proper drag is less understood by anglers than any other element of their fishing tackle. Proper drag is the amount of resistance which allows the fish to take line during sudden swift rushes, but allows the angler to retrieve line when the fish is less vigorous in its attempts to get away; it is the surging burst of power that determines if your drag is properly adjusted.

On some reels it frequently takes about twice as much force to start the drag slipping than is required once the spool starts to slip. A drag set at two pounds pull may require four or five pounds to start it. A properly adjusted drag is set for no more than a quarter of the test of the line.

An experienced angler will use the least amount of mechanical drag. If necessary, he'll use his fingers and hands for additional pressure. This is particularly true for ultra-light freshwater spinning. But too light a drag will also cause you to lose fish. The drag must be adjusted tightly enough to offer resistance when a fish strikes and you set the hooks.

A spinning reel should be filled to within $1/8$-inch of capacity for best casting and drag performance. The amount of line on the spool determines how much pull is required to make the spool slip. The less line, the greater the pull required. For this reason it is wise to lighten the drag. If the big fish you have hooked suddenly goes on a long run, as the fish is running, lighten the drag with your free hand.

A good drag must be adjustable and maintain its adjustment while fighting a fish; it must have a low starting ratio; it must release the line smoothly. High quality reels generally possess all these features, while cheap reels rarely do.

Here is a simple test to determine if your reel has a smooth drag: Thread the line through the rod guides and set the drag on a quarter of the line strength. Hold the rod butt at about a forty-five degree angle. Then ask your fishing buddy to run out with the line for fifty to a hundred yards. As the line starts out, your rod bends forward because of the greater pressure required to start the drag. The rod tip will then rise back to

running position. If the rod stays there and does not bounce around, the drag is smooth, but if the rod tip bounces and waves about like a willow branch in a high wind, your drag is poor and jerky.

Jerky drag may be caused by worn out washers or oil on the washers. Replace them. New reels sometimes also have jerky drags, and the drag must be broken in. Storing the reel with the drag on is one of the main reasons for poor performance. Drags are made of alternating soft and hard washers. If they are squeezed together for a long time, their life is shortened. After a day of fishing, release the tension on the drag so that the washers can return to their original shape. Maintain the drag on your reel properly and you'll be rewarded with bigger fish and more of them.

TIP NO. 12

Time and Fishing

At a certain reservoir in Texas, the local residents talk about a school of fish that lives under a bridge, much like the troll in the Billy Goat Gruff fairy tale. The fish don't eat goats, of course. Oh, they have been known to gobble a Lazy Ike dropped by some unsuspecting passerby now and again, but most of the time they mind their own business.

The fish are white bass and crappie and they appear beneath this bridge as regularly as clockwork almost every sunny

The drag on an open-faced spinning reel is adjusted by means of a spool nut on top of the spool.
The drag on some closed-faced spinning reels can be adjusted either by a micrometer ring just below the cone, or, as in this case, by a coin-slotted nut on the crank.

summer day between 10 A.M. and 2 P.M. Nobody has ever counted them but divers say they number in the thousands.

The fish are not as interested in the bridge as they are in its shadow; hence their appearance mostly on sunny days and at the time when the sun's rays penetrate deepest into the reservoir's clear water.

Sometimes this school provides good fishing, sometimes it does not. But that is not the point. What is important is how it demonstrates the importance of time. Time of day is more important and more complicated than most fishermen realize.

Time of day affects fish and fishermen in many ways, but the most obvious is through the light and heat of the sun.

Almost all fish are sensitive to light. For one thing, they don't have eyelids. For another, their skins are photosensitive — thanks to specialized cells concentrated mostly along the lateral line. Some fish are more sensitive than others. Walleye, for example, are highly sensitive. Catfish may be even more so. Some sunfish are relatively insensitive; the true bass seem to fall somewhere in between.

The fishermen must make use of this sensitivity. Clear, bright days make fishing for walleye and catfish tough, especially when there is no chop on the water. Waves distort the lens that is the water and prevent the sun's full rays from getting through. (Incidentally, most experienced anglers know that the best time to fish for walleye and catfish is at night; sensitivity to light is probably the reason.)

Seldom are bass found in very shallow water on those clear, bright, still days — at least not in lakes with clear water. This accounts, in part, for their tendency to make their forays into the shallows to feed in the early mornings and late evenings and, again, at night.

The heat of the sun also plays a role. Fish, being cold-blooded, control the temperature of their bodies by seeking out water they find most comfortable. When the rays of the sun warm the surface waters beyond their range of comfort, they leave. Generally water gets progressively warmer through the day until the late afternoon. Then it starts to cool again until, everything else being equal, the sun rises the next morning. Cooling takes place through contact with the air or by mixing with cooler water from below.

This warming-cooling cycle is responsible for many of the movements of fish. It accounts for summer fishing often being the best in the shallows early in the morning, when the water is at its coolest. It also accounts for fishing often not being too good on summer evenings — the water is usually still quite warm.

But heat and light do not tell the whole story. If they did, how could we account for those splurges of good fishing which sometimes come at odd hours of the day or night? Every experienced fisherman has seen these — they can come at midday in the summer when heat and light topside would seem to be unbearable.

Fish, like all living creatures, possess a body clock. They follow cycles which may or may not be synchronized with the sun.

They feed in cycles — studies conducted with aquariums have proved this, but just what triggers and regulates this phenomenon is poorly understood.

But I have not answered the most obvious question: When is the best time to go fishing? When you have time, of course.

TIP NO. 13

Anyone Can Catch Big Fish

The average Joe Fisherman thinks that catching a big fish depends mostly on luck. For Joe Fisherman this is true, but the real lunker hunters don't rely on luck. They fish for big fish.

Most fishermen fish for fun and generally catch the easiest fish to take — the average run-of-the-river specimens which are the most numerous. Sure, a big mossback largemouth may surge out of its den and lash at a spinner, or a big brook trout may come out of its hole and gently suck in a dainty dry fly, but this happens only rarely — only when Lady Luck has sat on your lap and kissed you.

The big fish specialist, the one who consistently brings in the lunkers, forgets about luck. He simply goes after big fish. You can too — if you are prepared to pay the price. And it is high. The big fish specialists seldom get any fast action. Theirs is the patient waiting game. They seldom catch fish on the surface, be they big bass with topwater plugs or big brook trout with dry flies, and they frequently get skunked. For these reasons, I am not a big specialist — I don't want to pay the price.

As a fish grows older and bigger, it changes its mode of living. It turns to deeper water and sticks closer to a lair of rocks, weeds, or sunken logs and stumps. It feeds mostly at night. The big specialists know this and they fish at night when most other fishermen are in bed.

Plumb the deep holes with big bait — giant streamers through dark holes, ten-inch plastic worms, or pork rind eels along reefs where the water drops off suddenly, or fish deep with big plugs. You won't catch many fish but the ones you do catch will be big ones. It all boils down to this: do you want more fish or big fish?

To catch big fish, you have to go after them. That means using big plugs, big spoons, and big flies. You have to be prepared to pay the price with fewer strikes and fewer fish, because big, old fish are not as abundant as smaller ones.

TIP NO. 14

Outfitting Your Tackle Box

What does a fisherman see when he looks at a new fishing lure? Different fishermen see different things. Some see little more than a hunk of plastic with hooks. They may admire its color, its finish, the shine on its hardware, but other than that they buy mostly on a lure's reputation, real or promoted. Other fishermen can see just by the design of a new fishing lure what it can do. They are like skilled woodworkers who can tell at a glance just what a certain chisel is designed for.

This, of course, is how everyone should look at a lure — not at its supposed miraculous qualities, not at its packaging, not even its price. There is no magic in any lure and they are all, even the best ones, nothing but tools.

This concept simplifies the problem for the fisherman who sets out to amass a well-stocked tackle box. Like a plumber or a carpenter, he should try to have all the tools he needs to perform all the situations he is likely to meet.

What are they? There are three basic situations — topwater, bottom-bumping, and in between. Within each of these categories are specialized tasks almost infinite in number. Sticking to these basics, each fisherman needs at least one topwater plug designed to float both at rest and on the retrieve. To the fish, it represents a large bug or wounded baitfish thrashing around on the surface. Topwater lures vary mainly in the way they create this illusion. They generally have a concave mouth which creates a bubble and a noise when they are moved. Other types of topwater plugs use spinners, diving planes, or flexible skirts. Some topwater plugs have no ornaments; nothing but hooks.

Bottom-bumping plugs are all alike in that they are designed to work along the bottom, plowing up mud to attract the fish's attention. The jig, merely a piece of lead to which a hook has been molded, is the classic bottom lure. All sorts of materials are attached to jigs to do different jobs: A piece of pork rind makes a jig an eel, a plastic worm makes a worm-jig, one large spinner makes a single-spin, two small spinners make a twin-spin. Skirts of feathers or hair or plastic enhance its appeal but it is still a jig, several of which should be in every tackle box.

The in-between lures are harder to choose and the variations are endless. They come in dozens upon dozens of shapes. Some sink at rest, some float. Some in-between lures overlap into the other two categories. In-between lures float at rest, but have a design that acts as a diving plane when retrieved. This design creates a wobble, known to fishermen as the plug's action. Most in-between lures have built-in action, a concept that probably was first developed in spoons.

There are other considerations. Every tackle box should have some weedless lures, at least one in each basic category. Some lures are designed to be fished rapidly, some slowly. To meet special needs the tackle box should contain some of both. Every box should have several sizes of spoons in silver and in gold.

TIP NO. 15

A Tool for the Tackle Box

One of the most useful tools to have in your tackle box is not even a fishing implement but surgical forceps, commonly called vein clamps by doctors. They are better for removing hooks deeply imbedded in a fish's gullet than long-nosed pliers or hook degorgers. The vein clamp is built like a pair of scissors, but the points are plier-shaped. The points can be locked into position.

Surgical forceps were designed for tough but delicate surgery and they are ideal for our purposes. To remove a hook reach deep into the throat cavity, lock on to the hook and carefully pry it free. Using this method the fish has a chance of surviving if you plan to release it. Even if it is going to wind up on your dinner plate, using the vein clamp is a much neater operation than the traditional method. Surgical vein clamps are easy to obtain. Many drug stores sell them, as do all medical and veterinary supply houses.

TIP NO. 16

Hone Your Hooks

It's difficult to say how many strikes or bites are missed because of dull hooks, but I'll bet that dull hooks outnumber all other reasons. So, hone your hooks regularly, certainly after every snag and after every three or four fish. The ideal hook sharpener is a three-sided jeweller's needle file. Your local jewellery store can get you one for about $1.50. Better still, order two, one for your tackle box, the other for your flyfishing vest. Tie it to your vest with a bit of old flyline.

TIP NO. 17

It's All in the Line

The line is an overlooked element in successful fishing. Much has been written about lures, flies, baits and tackle, but meaning rods and reels. And fishing talk always becomes lively when the merits (and demerits) of Kahle, Carlisle, Sproat, and Limerick hooks come to the fore.

But what about lines? In inches and feet they are more in the fish's home ground than lures, flies, baits, rods, reels, and hooks. If not chosen properly they do more to warn the fish than any other piece of equipment. The following story is a case in point.

Two friends are trolling for trout. They are using identical plugs. Both are tied to the spinning line with nickel snaps. But one is out-fishing the other four to one. Why, when they are using identical equipment?

Not so identical, it turns out. One is using four-pound line, the other eight. The trout see the heavier line and veer away from it. The four-pound test, like a cobweb in water, is nearly invisible.

When the loser switches to a four-pound spool, his strike percentage soars and gets even better when he trims down to a two-pound line. Lines are that important, but there are limits. Two-pound and four-pound lines are fine for small fish and rubble-free lakes, but they are almost worthless in good bass impoundments — stumps, sunken trees, weed beds and junky, rocky bottoms.

If a bass takes a half-hitch around a stump on a six-pound line, he is lost. He may be lost with an eight-pound too. Most bass fishermen use fourteen to twenty-pound line; if they feel a strike they really stick the fish — usually three times on the way to the boat. And they keep him moving, "disoriented," as they say. Some swing the fish from the water and toward the boat from twenty feet out. You can't do that with six-pound line, no matter what the weight of the bass.

Match the line weight to the situation and to the fish which you expect to catch. In Florida bass country, for example, you don't use a four-pound line. And you don't troll for muskies with eight-pound, either. On the other hand, fifteen-pound is heavy for bluegill, crappie and trout.

A light line lies easily on the water and casts effortlessly. It imparts more feel to light lures fished deeply. When a bass mouths such a lure, the fisherman knows immediately and can react instantly.

TIP NO. 18

It's Time We Changed Knots

If you, like most anglers, have been using a standard knot to tie on tippets or attach flies, hooks, lures, and swivels, you are in for a surprise. These knots are not as strong as you think. In fact, most of them have less than half the strength of the monofilament line with which they were tied.

This important discovery was made by two inquisitive Michigan fly fishermen, Don Schmidt and John Woodworth, with the backing of Leon Martuch, Chairman of the Board of Scientific Anglers Incorporated. Schmidt and Woodworth designed some testing equipment which simulated the sudden fast pull of a big fish as it strikes or suddenly takes off — the type of pull that causes lines to break.

They noticed that when a monofilament line breaks during a strike or a battle with a big fish, it nearly always breaks at the knot. Many anglers, myself included, always blamed this on a poorly tied knot or a worn tippet, or even carelessness in fighting the fish. No doubt many fish are lost for these reasons, but the old true blue knots are also to blame. They just aren't good enough.

What were Schmidt's and Woodworth's findings? They found that splicing knots, such as the blood knot and the double fisherman's knot, were very poor when compared to lesser-known knots such as the double nail or improved blood knot. Their findings for attaching knots were equally revealing. The well-known clinch knot and the double turle were not nearly as strong as the clinch knot two times through or the improved clinch knot. And they found that all knots improved in strength if they were thoroughly tightened, dispelling the notion that the hooked fish will tighten the knot.

The following diagrams show how to tie the stronger knots. My fishing hat is off to you, Messrs. Schmidt and Woodworth. You performed a valuable service for us.

THE DOUBLE NAIL KNOT

Overlap the ends of your two strands that are to be joined and twist them together about ten turns.

Separate one of the center twists and thrust the two ends through the space, as illustrated.

Pull together and trim off the short ends.

THE IMPROVED BLOOD KNOT

Thrust end of line through eye of hook and double back. Loop around standing part of line five or six times.

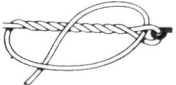

Thrust end back up between the eye and the coils, then back through the big loop.

Pull up tight and trim end.

THE IMPROVED CLINCH KNOT

Twist looped end five or six turns around main line, then pass through loop at hook, and back up through big loop spanning knot.

Tighten knot slowly and trim.

THE DOUBLE IMPROVED CLINCH KNOT

TIP NO. 19

The Uni-Knot — an Easy Knot for All Fishing

One of the easiest and fastest knots ever has been developed to meet virtually every knot need for either fresh or saltwater fishing — from tying hook to line to joining lines, tying leaders, forming a double-line shock leader, to even snelling a hook.

This single-knot system is the brainchild of Victor Dunaway, the editor of *Florida Sportsman* magazine and author of numerous books on knots and fishing techniques.

Described for the first time in *Sports Afield* magazine, Dunaway's Uni-Knot has been tested in hundreds of variations by the Du Pont Company. They found that the Uni-Knot consistently holds from ninety-five to one hundred percent of the pound-test breaking strength of the line.

"I didn't invent the knot," explains Vic Dunaway. "It evolved from tedious testing of known but helter-skelter knot-tying principles. The actual configuration has been used in the past for the solitary purpose of forming the Norm Duncan Loop, to attach free-swinging flies and other lures to monofilament leader. Starting from this base, it was a matter of hundreds of trial-and-error attempts to adapt the same knot to each different situation."

To learn this system, the fisherman must first master the basic Uni-Knot, as used to tie line to the eye of a hook, swivel, or lure. Here are the steps:

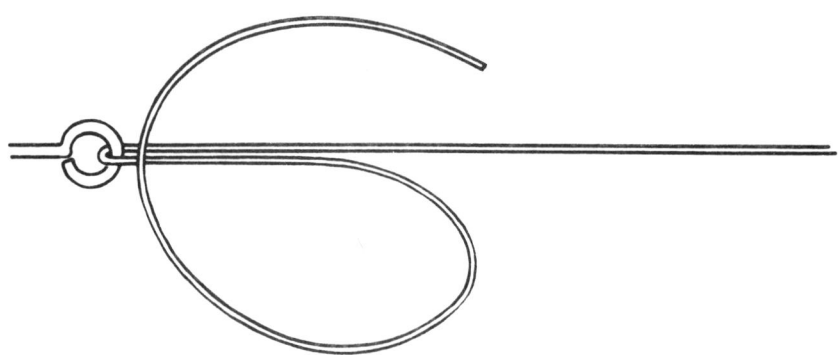

Run the line through the eye for at least six inches. Fold it back to form a double line and make a circle back toward the hook or lure with the tag end.

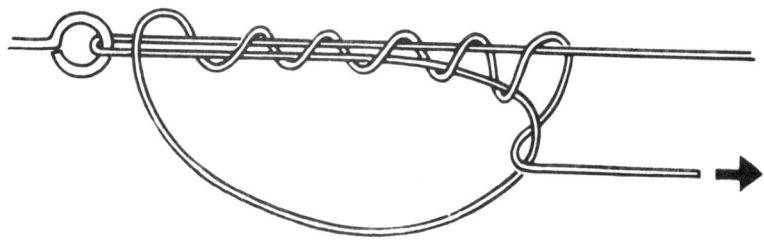

Make six turns with the tag end around the double line and through the circle. Holding the double line at the point where it passes through the eye, pull the tag end, as indicated by the arrow, until the six turns are snugged into a tight barrel.

Now, grasp the standing part of the line and pull (see arrow) to slide the knot up against the eye.

Continue to pull standing line until knot is tight. You can trim the tag end flush with the closest coil of the knot, because the Uni-Knot doesn't allow line slippage.

To tie a small loop into the eye of a lure or fly giving it free movement in the water, tie the same knot up to the point where the turns are snugged around the standing line.

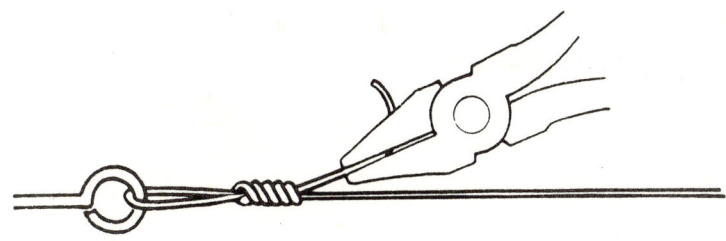

Next, slide the knot toward the eye of the lure by pulling on the standing line, until the desired loop size. Use tackle box pliers to hold the knot at this point, pulling the tag end to maximum tightness.

The loop will hold under normal casting and retrieving conditions. Once a fish is hooked, the knot will slide tight against the eye for better security. In the Du Pont tests, for instance, a pressure of about five pounds on a fourteen-pound test line was required to pull up the loop.

In joining two lines of about the same diameter, the Uni-Knot offers a much easier solution than the rather difficult blood knot, yet is every bit as strong. First, overlap the ends of the lines, about six inches. Form the Uni-Knot circle with one of the ends, crossing the two lines at about half the overlapped distance.

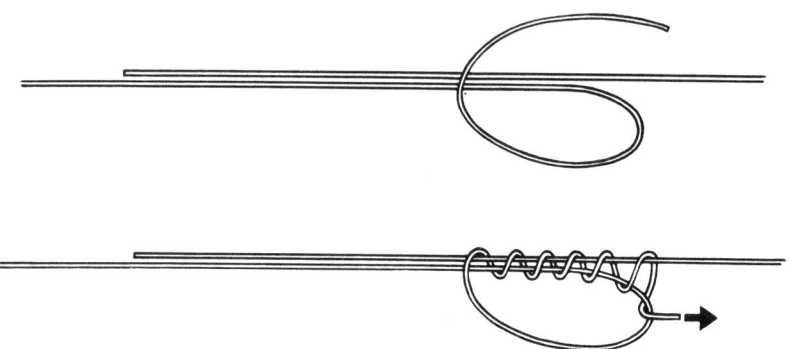

Make six turns around the two lines and through the circle, as in the basic knot. Pull tag end in direction indicated by the arrow to snug knot tight up around the other line.

This will leave the other half of the overlap unknotted. Using loose end of overlapped line, tie another Uni-Knot and snug up.

Now, pull the two standing lines in opposite directions (as shown by arrows) to slide the knots together.

Pull as tight as possible and snip off ends close to the nearest coil. Tied with single lines, this knot does not test one hundred percent of the line strength, breaking frequently at just over ninety percent. By doubling both ends of the lines to be joined and tying Uni-Knots with the double lines, it achieves a hundred percent. The single-line knot, however, is strong enough for all practical situations.

To tie on a leader that is no more than four times the pound test of the line, double the end of the line and overlap this loop of line and the leader for about a six-inch length. Treating the doubled line as though it were a single strand, tie the basic Uni-Knot around the leader, using only three turns through the circle. Next, tie a Uni-Knot with the leader around the doubled line, again using only three turns. Pull them together and trim the ends as before.

If the leader material is five times the pound test of the line, or larger, the knot is even easier. Double ends of both line and heavy leader back about six inches. Slip the loop of line through the loop of leader, far enough to permit tying a Uni-Knot around both strands of leader, using three turns through the circle. With finger through loop of line, pull the knot tight around both strands of leader. Finally, with one hand, pull only the standing leader (not both strands) while you pull both strands of the line with the other hand. Pull until the knot slides to the end of the leader loop; then continue pulling until all slippage is gone. Trim off all loose ends.

To tie monofilament leader to a flyline, the Uni-Knot can be used to tie a nail knot, without using a nail. With the butt end of the leader, form a Uni-Knot circle, overlapping the end of the fly line and taking four or more turns through the circle. Tighten the knot rather loosely. Because of the flyline's soft coating, coils of the knot must be tightened by degrees, prodding them together with thumb nail while doing so. For final tightening, grip short end of leader with pliers and pull hard enough to make the knot bite into the coating of the flyline. Trim with nail clippers.

The Uni-Knot can even be used in forming a double-line shock leader, replacing the difficult Bimini Twist or the Spider Hitch. Clip off enough line to form a doubled loop of the length desired. Tie the ends of this piece with an overhand knot, which will later be clipped off. Double the end of the standing line and overlap about six inches of the knotted end of the loop piece. Form a Uni-Knot circle with the tied end of the doubled piece, and make four wraps around the doubled standing line. Pull this knot tight around both strands. Reverse the procedure, making a Uni-Knot with the loop of standing line around the doubled piece, again taking four turns. Holding both strands of standing line in one hand and both strands of the doubled piece in the other, pull the knots together until they barely touch. Now, snug up as tight as possible, pulling both strands of the doubled piece but only the main strand of standing line. Trim off all excess tag ends.

Snelling a hook with the Uni-Knot is a bonus, because it permits making a snell with the end of the line rather than a piece of leader material.

Insert the line or leader through the hook eye for about six inches and form the Uni-Knot circle. Make as many turns through the loop and around the line and hook shank as desired. (Four or five are enough.) Close the knot by pulling on the short end of line, but there is no need to snug the wraps up at this point.

Finish tightening by pulling the standing line in one direction and the hook in the other.

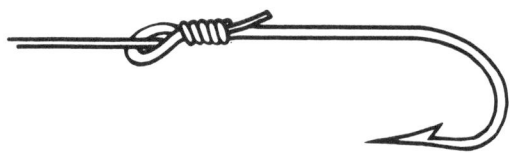

TIP NO. 20

For Trout — Flyfish the Edges

On a strange stream one question in every angler's mind is: How do I fish this stream? To become enamored with a stream the first time you wade in is typical, but a successful affair with a trout is something else.

Approach a stream intending to fish the edges — a simple way to read the water, find out where the trout are, and whether to use a dry, wet or nymph or bucktail fly. Stream edges are trout feeding areas. They are pockets of slower water behind obstructions that break the current. Edges may be corners in the stream flow created by the meandering bends, the bottoms, or overhanging foliage.

Among the most obvious places to fish are rocks with ample vertical surface to break the flow of water. Rocks get pages of print in angling texts, rightly so, and it pays to work a fly well in the current edges created by a rock. Trout rest in quiet water behind them. They may also move out to the sides or in front to actively feed in buffers of water where the current has slowed.

Where two currents flow together in a "V" is another good edge. Stand upstream and let a weighted fly hang below you, weaving in the mixing waters. Dart it upstream and let it drift back down. This simple method unnerves trout. Where a side channel enters the main stream is a good "V". On the stream, currents mix and dig out holes; such holes may be holding or feeding stations for trout.

The incoming riffle to a pool creates one and sometimes two productive edges. The sloping drop-off sometimes holds the largest trout in the open water off the pool. A sunken nymph or bucktail that scratches along the bottom through the head of the pool is good for hooking trout. In low, clear water trout will rise to a dry fly. A floater is often a good choice on the second of the hot spots — the corner of slack water on the shallow side at the head of a pool. Similarly, a trout often lies in the shallows on the inside of an even flowing bend, downstream from the point of land.

Trout find where a current begins to curve away from the main flow, such as an eddy the size of a desk top. Larger back eddies form congregating places for pecking orders of trout. Trout feed at the lower end of a pool, where the main flow flattens and fans out.

Keep an eye out for underwater rocks along the choppy-faced waters. Many anglers pass up such broken water, but the trout in these pockets rise to a dry fly floated on the bouncing water or on the seam of flat water along the edges.

Banks are extremely good edges. Slide short casts across the stream and underbrush so that a well-greased, hairwing dry fly bobs downstream like a grasshopper or a stonefly. On slow, flat water a small fly on a long, light leader may be the ticket. Even dropping a fly on a short line in front of a bush can lure edgy trout. Overhanging banks, with only a single branch for added shade, may hide the best trout of the day.

It's worth your time to explore the side channels and spring-fed tributaries along a stream. Sometimes I have enjoyed better fishing on such stream fingers than on the main stream, and these forks offer their own edges for fish.

Cast again and again to edges where you believe a trout is waiting. You'll need to develop confidence in fishing blind in order to work such spots but edges of currents, like signs along the road, will guide you.

To trout, stream edges such as pockets of slower water behind obstructions, incoming riffles, undercut or overgrown banks are all top feeding areas. That's where an angler should fish.

TIP NO. 21

The Myth of the Long Cast

One of the great flyfishing myths is the long cast. The myth is this: in order to catch trout you must be able to cast out ninety feet of line without even blinking an eyelash. Nothing is farther from the truth. Being able to cast long distances will, of course, help you take more fish but only on big rivers or on bonefish flats, and then only if you've got other flyfishing skills to back up your casting ability.

The long cast has disadvantages. The long length of line on the current can make the fly drag and either snatch the fly away from the fish or put it down. Dropping a long length of line across a pool and hauling it back may spook fish. Or, when a fish does take a fly on a long line, it may let go before you can straighten the line to set the hook.

Most of our trout streams can be fished successfully with short casts — thirty feet or a bit more. Even when fish are rising across a pool, you can frequently wade within casting distance. Trout sucking off the surface have a small field of vision. You have to cast precisely to get them and a short cast is more accurate. It also allows you to set the hook more quickly, ensuring a greater percentage of fish hooked.

Don't despair if you can't cast a great distance; there are many of us in the same boat. Get as close to the fish or fish-holding water as possible, then cast with pinpoint accuracy.

One of the great myths about flyfishing is that only the angler who can make a long cast will catch fish. That may be true on big rivers, but on most trout streams a short-cast flyfisherman will do just as well.

TIP NO. 22

Nymph + Dry Fly = Trout!

Each trout season you can't pick up an outdoor magazine and read about trout fishing without coming across something about nymphs.

There are, literally, dozens of ways in which a nymph may be fished, but tyro nymph fishermen are advised to watch the leader or the tip of the flyline and to set the hook immediately at the first sign of movement. Why? Because a trout does not strike at a nymph as it would a streamer or dry fly. Instead, it just opens its mouth and sucks it in as it drifts helplessly with the current. Often the type of water you're fishing makes it difficult to even know you're getting a strike until after the trout has rejected your offering. This is especially true when fishing a swift, turbulent run, or late in the evening when it's difficult to see the leader or the flyline.

My most effective method when using nymphs is to use a high-floating, bright yellow dry fly off a dropper. The nymph drifts freely at the end of the leader and, even if a tiny chub nudges the nymph, the dry fly is immediately pulled under, indicating a strike. Your reflexes take over and, in an instant, you lift back and are fast to a tail-walking rainbow or a tough, sulking brown.

What type of fly should you use off the dropper? An Irresistible is a fine dry fly for this. It is easy to see and floats high. I've used it often off the dropper. A Bivisible is a good choice too. In bright yellow it looks like anything but an aquatic insect but, surprisingly, I've caught many trout on these dries which were simply acting as a signal float to the primary nymph at the end of a fine tippet. Indeed, I've hooked and landed a trout on the nymph and on the dry at the same time — and on several occasions at that!

Maintaining good control of the nymph-and-dry combination is easy on an eight or nine-foot-long leader, with the dropper about a foot from the end of the flyline. The key is to use a stiffish piece of leader material to tie in the blood knot that will keep the dropper out and away from the leader and minimize tangling. Too light or too soft a leader can cause problems.

I've used all the generally accepted nymphing techniques with this combination, in all kinds of water, and caught trout in a ridiculously easy manner. Keep the nymph deep. Be sure to throw several mends into the line, thus permitting an absolutely free float, with no drag whatsoever on the nymph and dry fly combination floating along. But don't some natural nymphs have locomotion of their own? Yes, a few do. But most drift freely with the current. The closer you can imitate this free-drifting with your nymphs, the more apt you are to hook trout.

TIP NO. 23

Nymphs and Streamers Are Trout Favorites

Peek over the shoulder of any experienced trout angler as he opens a fly box and you're bound to see a wide assortment of nymphs and streamers. In the Catskills, these two types of patterns rank as the year-round favorites. Trout can't seem to resist a well-presented nymph and at the very least they will dart out to investigate a streamer as it swims by their lie.

Streamers are further categorized as those that imitate natural bait in the streams or ponds (called imitators) and those that tend to arouse the curiosity of a fish (called attractors). As a matter of fact, some anglers prefer to start with an attractor pattern to locate the fish and then switch over to a nymph to tease the fish into striking. Nymphs are an intermediate stage of insect development. When the time comes for the nymph to change — to hatch into an adult insect — it rises to the surface of the water. The rise triggers trout to action.

It is much easier to fish a streamer than a nymph and the technique can be acquired quickly. If you're fishing a stream, study the waters carefully and try to determine where a trout would most likely reside. It's important to approach the stream cautiously below the fish and keep low to minimize your silhouette. Streamers are particularly effective in fast water — the cast should be made up and across the moving water.

As the current carries the offering downstream, keep a tight line so you can feel the strike. Just as the fly makes a wide swing at the end of the arc of line, start retrieving in short, sporadic darts by stripping line. Frequently however, you'll get a strike on the swing as the fish scampers to catch the eluding meal. Streamers also work well in the deeper spots, but you should let them sink slightly before retrieving. Then, work them toward you slowly and get ready.

Polaroid sunglasses help to see underwater; you should be able to catch a glimpse of the "flash" as a trout leaves its hiding place to strike. If it misses the streamer, it will return to the original lie. You can either make another cast or switch to a nymph and float it by. As fish always face into the current, the fly should pass in front of it for best results.

Fishing a nymph properly is an art. In a stream, it can be fished up-current and allowed to float freely. You'll have to keep a tight line and watch the tip of the line for a signal of the strike. Trout don't wallop nymphs. Instead, they merely inhale them and you have to be quick to set the hook. The instant you see the end of the flyline pull even slightly, lift the rod.

In deeper pools or ponds weighted nymphs are the number one artificial. You can fish them with a floating flyline, but let them sink. Then retrieve very slowly, barely moving the fly. The slightest bump is a strike, and it usually happens without warning.

If you've finished the retrieve without a strike, wiggle the rod tip from side to side as you lift it slowly for another cast. This causes the nymph to scamper toward the surface like an insect about to take off. If a trout sees it, you can bet he'll never turn it down.

Whether you prefer a nymph or a streamer or a combination of both, they will account for more trout than all of the other flies combined — and they work from early spring until late fall.

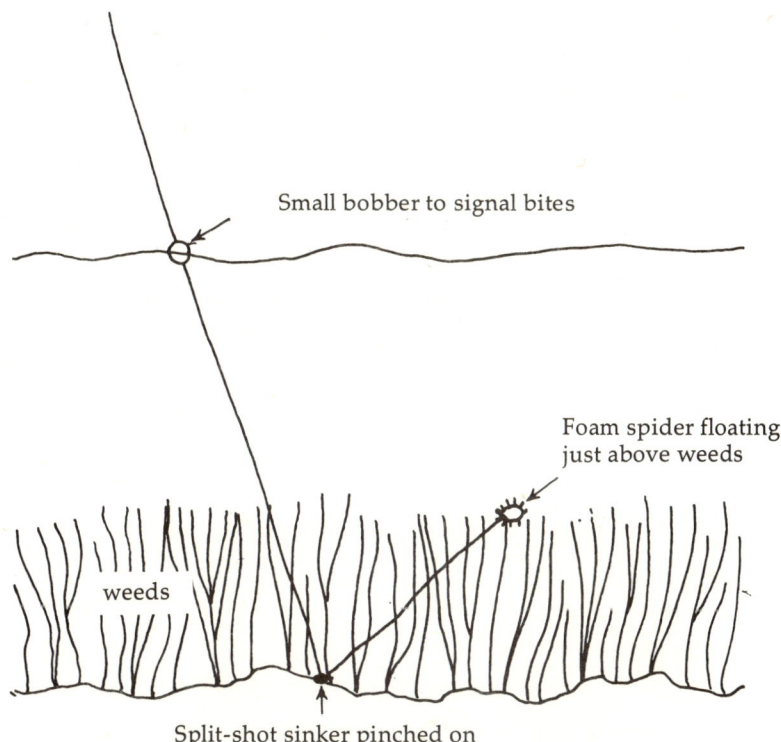

Small bobber to signal bites

Foam spider floating just above weeds

weeds

Split-shot sinker pinched on line at a depth that will make spider float just above weeds

TIP NO. 24

Drifting Them Deep

During the early spring, fall and winter, the waters of many streams are low and crystal clear. But during spring run-off, the story is different. Spring run-off can turn a river into a raging torrent that tears the free-stone beds into short, deep holes and long, shallow runs. River banks are steep and heavily wooded. These conditions, coupled with a year-round fishing season, have spawned as skillful a group of fast-water, short-line nymph fishermen as you'll find anywhere. Here I must mention Chuck Fothergill, for if this is anyone's technique, it is his.

There is nothing exotic about the equipment. A $7^1/_2$ to $8^1/_2$-foot rod, a double-tapered floating line, good line floatant, a twelve to fifteen-foot leader (the longer preferred), lead weight, and weighted nymphs.

The junction of the line to the leader must be smooth, as you will very often fish so close that the end of the line will be drawn into the tip of the rod. A Nail Knot covered with several coats of Pliobond Cement is the simplest to prepare and as efficient as any.

The line should be well dressed immediately before fishing and often enough throughout the day to keep it right on top. A good stiff leader is needed to turn the weight over.

For weight, Twist-Ons are best. These are lead strips packaged like matches in a matchbook. A half strip at a time is wrapped as smoothly as possible on the leader, the first about eighteen inches from the nymph. The ends are carefully pressed down so as not to catch the line or leader in passing on the false casts. A good pinch with the fingernail will secure it tightly to the leader. If additional weight is needed, half strips are added, each about five inches up the leader from the last. Spreading the weight like this allows for more ease in casting, and exact control of the amount of weight.

The amount of weight to be used is easily determined. Start with a half weight. If unsuccessful, continue adding half weights until a fish or the bottom is caught. If the bottom, remove a half weight and the nymph will be drifting right off the bottom. The tippet should be about eighteen inches long, and in clear water as fine as 5x.

Cast upstream so the nymph will dead drift downstream naturally with as little drag as possible. And now — the hardest idea to get across: the line must be tight. The nymph is under water and the only indication of a strike will be a slight movement upstream or a subtle hesitation of the floating portion of the line. Slack will prevent the interruption of the drift being transmitted to the surface. When fishing very close, there will be no line out of the rod, and you must watch the tension on the leader. It is true that a rock or branch will cause the same reaction as a strike; one does "catch" a lot of such things.

Ideas to keep in mind:
- The line *must* be floating and tight. It is better to have a line that is a little too tight — that is, influencing the drift of the nymph to some degree — than to have it too slack.
- Slack will not get the nymph down; weight will.
- Concentrate on the visible part of the line (or leader) and react instantly to the least hint of hesitation.

Proficiency in all methods of fishing requires casting ability, water reading ability, and knowledge of available types of food. When "drifting them deep" another skill is needed: sensing that hidden strike. Few experiences can be as rewarding as when a sixth sense tells you "that's it," and it is — a fighting trout from the deep.

TIP NO. 25

Weighted Flies for Fast Water

If you have trouble getting your flies to sink deep enough to reach trout on the bottom of wild water, weight your flies down with lead. Here's how it's done.

Wrap soft lead wire, available in hardware and hobby shops, right around the body of whatever fly you are using. Any fly — a nymph, streamer, or bucktail — can be weighted. The lead wire will not slide down the fly body and interfere with the barb and point of the hook.

Lead strips or split-shot attached to leaders will also sink your fly, but they are much harder to cast with a flyrod because of the uneven distribution of the weight. A weighted fly handles much better.

The lead wire also gives a segmented look to the fly's body, similar to the look of many insects in the larval and nymph stages. The natural dull gray of the lead wire is fine, but it is also a good idea to have other colors — green, red, yellow, and so on. The lead wire is easy to paint once it has been wrapped around the fly's body.

Although weighted flies are made with fast, deep water in mind, they can be used successfully in deep pools and lakes. If you've got deep water, wrap your flies with lead.

TIP NO. 26

Get to Know the Caddis

Caddis flies, sometimes known as sedge, are among the most common and widely distributed of aquatic insects. With over nine hundred species, caddis outnumber mayflies by a wide margin, but little is known of caddis by the average flyfisherman. Until quite recently little information was available. Schwiebert's *Match the Hatch* devoted four pages to the entire order. Flick's *Streamside Guide* never mentions caddis at all. However, Wright's *Fishing the Dry Fly as a Living Insect*, and Schwiebert's *Nymphs* have shed considerable light on the subject. Both are recommended reading.

While it is not necessary to be able to identify all nine hundred species, understanding the basic life cycle of the caddis is important in order to imitate it successfully. Unlike mayflies and stoneflies, the caddis has a complete life cycle. Eggs deposited in the water hatch into worm or grub-like larvae. Caddis larvae are divided into groups — those that build protective cases and those that range freely over the stream bed without cases. Cased larvae build their shelter of tiny pebbles, sand, sticks, leaf fragments. The cases of the various genera are distinctively their own.

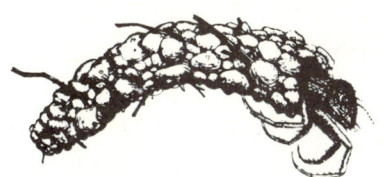

Caddis larva in case

Cased caddis are commonly known as stick worms, caddis worms, and caddis creepers. Of the larvae that do not build cases, some are known as net spinners. The net spinners build unique net systems among the rocks of the stream bed to collect food and to provide shelter. The caddis larvae that do not build cases are more readily available to trout and are more easily imitated by the fly tyer.

The second stage of caddis development is known as a pupa. The pupa stage comes when the larvae are fully grown and is similar to the change caterpillars undergo when changing to chrysalis and then to butterflies. The caddis larva seals itself in the case or spins a silk-like cocoon for this change to take place.

Caddis larva

Once pupation is complete (it can take two weeks or longer), the pupa breaks out of the case or cocoon and swims to the

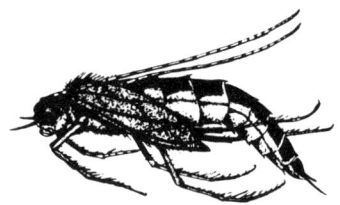

Caddis pupa

surface to hatch. Some slow-water species do crawl to shallow water and hatch like stoneflies: by crawling out of the water on to rocks, plant reeds, or on deadfalls.

As a general rule, to hatch, slow-water species crawl out of the water; swift-water species swim to the surface. Whichever, the pupa stage is when the trout has its best chance at a caddis feast.

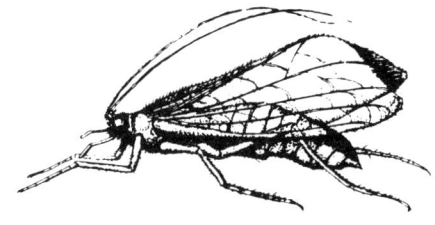

Caddis adult

Adult caddis flies are at first clumsy fliers and will often make several attempts at flight, making them easy targets for trout. Egg-laying caddis will also trigger eager rises. Len Wright's *Fishing the Dry Fly as a Living Insect*, describes fishing the dry caddis fly (fluttering caddis) in detail. His technique is deadly and every dry fly man should be well versed with it.

TIP NO. 27

Caddis Techniques

Over the past few years, I have found that the caddis, in particular my variation of the Turkeywing caddis, has been my most consistent pattern. I have learned, however, that it is not always successful when consistently fished in the same way. Every situation requires a slightly different tactic. After reviewing my log, I have come up with a few tactics which I hope will be helpful.

- Fish across or downstream — in general I fish the caddis either directly across or downstream. This gives you much better control should you want to impart action to the fly.
- Try skating the fly — caddis are rarely at rest on the water and are usually bouncing along. Vary your movements from a slight twitch to foot-long skates.
- Use a good fly floatant — one of the most important things to remember when fishing the caddis is to keep it high and dry so that it can be manoeuvered easily. I have found Gehrke's Gink hard to beat. It pays to dry the fly and redress it frequently for best results.
- Use a long and fine leader — the longest leader and finest tippet you can handle. This not only minimizes the chances of spooking the fish, but also enables you to present your fly and manoeuver it as naturally as possible.

- Use a medium-short fast action rod — I use a rod between six and seven feet long with a fast, crisp action. I find I have much better loop control and casting accuracy with this type of rod. Also, a shorter rod is much less tiring to use than a long one.
- Try fishing it wet — after you have fished your fly until it is dragged under, try fishing it wet for a few feet. At times when I cannot get a fish to take on the surface, it will be murdered at the end of the swing after submerging.
- Don't ignore riffles and pocket water — in the summer and fall some of the most consistent hot spots are in the riffles and pocket water. These areas provide more cover and oxygen for the fish during low water. Make sure your fly is well dressed.
- Try to hit the fish on the head — there are times when the only way you can get a feeding fish to take is to cast directly to the rise (hit him on the head). Be ready, however, because when it takes it's like an explosion; if you miss you seldom get a second chance.
- Fish the obstacles — don't ever pass up rocks, brush, treefalls without at least a few casts and twitches of a caddis. The two biggest fish I took this year came fishing blindly to overhanging brush and a twitching fly.

If I had only one dry fly to use it would be the Turkeywing caddis. I have used it consistently all season long with good results by experimenting with different methods of skating the caddis.

TIP NO. 28

The Latex Caddis

Like a whole trainload of other anglers, I've been suckered with eleven dozen new super flies and gimmicks that were supposed to be the final solution for this or that fishing situation. Fly tyers and writers become absolutely unglued when they are telling you about the new version of the Royal Coachman that they have just created. You know — the one that features six turns of hackle instead of five. Well, new wrinkles come and go like the seasons and after the smoke clears away, it's back to basics. We rediscover that the old Light Cahil, Adams, and Wooley Worm continue to perform admirably on just about every stream in the nation.

But ——- ! I've recently been introduced to a super nymph that catches fish like crazy. A fellow with the improbable name of Raleigh Boaze who lives in Frederick, Maryland, sent me some funny-looking little bugs that are made from white latex rubber. The idea is, if you haven't already guessed it, to suggest the shucked out version of a caddis worm. Caddis flies in some form or another are reasonably common on most of the trout streams of the East and not a few Western waters. About the only basic difference in the Eastern and Western versions is the size; some of the Western caddis flies are truly monstrous.

Most of the time the fisherman sees the caddis as an adult. It's tough to spot in its larval stage because of the well-camouflaged stick and stone house that it builds around itself. When a gob of small stones and twigs is found in a trout's stomach, it's safe to assume it was eating caddis worms— case and all. We don't often see the caddis worm without its case, but the trout must know what it looks like because they will actually pick these imitations up and move away with them — the soft feel of the latex rubber fools them completely.

Raleigh sent me a few samples tied on accentuated English bait hooks, and I must admit they look and are good. Trouble is, they may be too effective and the pronounced curve of the hook makes it difficult to release fish that you don't wish to kill. I've been winding these worms on Mustad's 3399 hook and pinching the barbs down, but almost any medium to heavy-weight hook would work as long as it has a Sproat or similar bend.

Here's how you make it:

Select a hook that's about the size of the caddis worms in your stream and cover the shank with cream-colored floss. Extend the floss to well into the bend of the hook.

Cut a strip of latex rubber about an eighth of an inch wide and tie it on at the bend. Wind forward, keeping a bit of tension on the rubber and lay the wraps on in such a way that there is a slight taper from tail to head.

Allow enough room at the head end to make two wraps of dark brown chenille. Whip finish, apply a spot of cement, and that's it.

Where do you get the latex? Make friends with someone who supplies such materials to hospitals or, in a pinch, ask some doctor friend for a discarded pair of surgical gloves. This rubber is a bit thin, but it will work.

The result is an extremely realistic, slightly off-white worm, with a soft, lifelike texture. Fished with a sinktip line on a sensitive rod, this is a bottom-bouncing creation that can be an ace in the hole on difficult days. The trout won't rise to eat the worm, but they will pick it up from the bottom. I suppose you could use a piece of wraparound sinker to get it down, but the sinking line is much easier to use. Besides, I hate to put sinkers on a tapered leader.

TIP NO. 29

Catching Trophy Bass

Catching a big, mounting-sized largemouth is easier than you think. All it takes is some know-how on where and how to fish.

Let's take the where part first. What constitutes a trophy bass is relative. For example, a seven or eight-pound bass from Michigan or Minnesota, indeed from the entire bass range of the northern United States and Canada, is a bass to be proud of. But it would take a largemouth of ten or eleven pounds before you could call it a trophy fish in the mid-South. On the other hand, you would have to add another two to three pounds to that fish to call it a trophy bass in southern California or Florida, where a ten-pound largemouth is bragging size, but nothing to eulogize in story and song.

The reason is simple. Fish do not grow, or grow very little, once the water turns cold — in winter. The shorter the winter, the longer the growing season. In the Deep South, where there is no really cold winter weather, fish grow the year round. A fish grows all its life. It may not grow quite as rapidly as it gets older, but it does grow.

There are many top-producing bass lakes in Florida that have only fifteen to twenty feet of water, or lakes in Minnesota that never go over thirty feet, but these lakes seldom produce big bass. Most trophy bass come from lakes that have sixty to eighty feet of water. Generally, these deep lakes are not quite as fertile and hence not as productive as the shallower lakes. The deep lakes will have fewer fish per acre. The fish will be a bit slower-growing, but they will be bigger than in the shallower lakes with their heavy bass populations. Lakes that are known for big bass are generally well-known to biologists of the state or provincial game department. This is where you should begin your search. Outdoor writers in local papers may also be of help.

Once you've found the big bass lake, you still have to find where to fish, where the old mossbacks hang out. Eliminate all the really deep water — a hundred feet or more — in the center of the lake. Chances are this area is fishless because of no oxygen, no cover, and mostly a mud bottom. Avoid the shallow inshore water of less than thirty feet as well. Concentrate on water with sudden drop-offs, water with, say, fifty to sixty feet of depth and still plenty of cover in the form of stumps, logs, or boulders where a big bass might have its lair. Look for small, deep holes. A depth finder or fish locator is an invaluable instrument for finding the type of habitat that attracts big bass.

The second thing to remember is that bass prefer water temperatures between 68°F. and 73°F. They will abandon old haunts if the water temperature rises above 75°F. or falls below 50°F. Recent feeding experiments have shown that bass feed most vigorously between 70°F. and 73°F.

Once you have pinpointed the promising spots, begin fishing. Forget about little tidbits. Big bass don't care much for hors d'oeuvres. They want big meals, so give them large lures or chunks of big bait. Big jigging spoons bounced off the bottom, big jigs with a chunk of pork rind, big plastic worms, and big pork rind eels are all good. The trick is to get the lure near the fish. Big bass are lazy. They won't move too far to take the bait.

Use a stout rod with plenty of backbone, but one with a sensitive tip so that you can feel the instant the bass sucks in the lure.

Use heavy line — no less than twenty pounds. Many of the Deep South big bass fishermen prefer twenty-five or even thirty-pound line. Use a strong reel with a good drag. A casting reel with a star drag is best.

TIP NO. 30

Ripping for Bass

Every good bass tournament professional has a few tricks up his sleeve when the usual tactics don't work. Tom Mann, a top tournament bass fisherman, discovered the trick of moving his lure as fast as he could when conventional retrieves brought no action. He called it "ripping," probably because it really ripped the water. It didn't take long for the competition to spot this trick when he wiped their eyes on generally unproductive days. Once they began to use it, the trick petered out, but ripping is still not widely known except in the bassiest of bass circles in the Deep South.

The technique is simple. Fire out a long cast and let the lure settle to the bottom. Your line always goes slack when the lure hits the bottom. Reach to the water with your rod tip and reel in all the slack line. Then, whip your rod back over your head as fast as you can and reel it in at the same time. This will jerk the lure off the bottom and propel it rapidly through the water.

When, briefly, your rod has been over your head, lower the rod tip to the water and let the lure settle to the bottom again. Keep repeating this cycle until you work the lure to the boat or shore.

Generally bass strike the lure when it is moving, but they may wait until it stops. Don't think for a minute that the lure is moving too fast for a bass to catch. When the old bronzeback wants to, he can move with tremendous speed.

To rip the lure properly you have to equip yourself for the task. Bass tournament pros use a fairly stiff $7\ 1/2$-foot saltwater spinning rod with a high ratio retrieve saltwater spinning reel. The reel is always filled to within an eighth of an inch of the spool's edge with twenty-pound mono. Such a reel filled to capacity will bring in thirty inches of line for every turn of the handle. Also, the fairly heavy line backed with the stiff rod will have plenty of muscle to horse out snags.

Lure selection is also important. Although most sinking lures can be used, the best are plugs that have a big lip for bottom-bumping. Jigs, well dressed with bucktail or perhaps a spinner blade on the hook, are also good.

Why do bass strike at such rapidly propelled lures? It is an enigma. One theory is the angler reflex. The bass just don't like this fast-moving critter going by a lair. Ripping doesn't always work, but then nothing does in fishing. It seems to work best in waters where bass get pounded fairly heavily

with lures fished in standard ways, and they may be a bit lure-shy under such circumstances. A lure ripped through the water doesn't look like just another piece of hardware: it doesn't give the bass any time to be lure-shy.

If you are a dedicated bass man, give ripping a try. On some days it may bring in the bacon — I mean the bass.

TIP NO. 31

Bass Bugging on Lakes or Ponds

Both large and smallmouth bass follow a well-established annual pattern in deep lakes and reservoirs. They move into the shallow water near shore when it warms up in the spring and they remain there until after spawning. When the shallows begin to get uncomfortably warm, they drift back out and down, until they find the water temperature that suits them. This may be from fifteen to thirty feet beneath the surface; nearly always close to a rock, sand, or gravel bottom.

As the water cools in the autumn, they may move inshore again. Then, as it begins to get uncomfortably cold in the late fall, they move into deeper water once more. On some lakes, even during the hottest weather, they come into the shallows to feed at night, returning to the depths during the day. This is

A super-fast retrieving technique developed by Tom Mann, the bass tournament pro, is proving to be a good way to catch all bass — largemouths and smallmouths — even in the Ojibway fishing country of Canada. Mann calls the technique "ripping" and recommends a 7½-foot rod and high-ratio retrieve saltwater spinning reel.

When you take a kid out fishing, don't coach or be overly helpful. Let mistakes happen, but make the fishing trip an enjoyable experience.

not the case everywhere, but where it is, you catch bass on bugs late in the evening, at night, and early in the morning all through the summer.

The knowledge of where bass are most likely to be at any particular time is the key to catching them in deep lakes and reservoirs. Fish the shoreline in spring and early summer, going deeper and deeper as the surface water gets warmer. Try the shoreline again in the autumn, then start fishing deeper once more as the water grows colder on top.

The time to fish a bass bug is when the bass are in shallow water. You can wade, casting ahead, or fish from a boat, moving along slowly at a comfortable casting distance from shore. Only rarely are long casts necessary; accurate casts are.

Bass like cover. Drop your bug close to lily pads, reeds, brush, logs, rocks — anything that might be a hiding place. Let it float motionless until the rings die away. Then give it a sharp jerk by briskly raising the rod tip. The bug shouldn't move more than a few inches, but the movement should be quick enough to make it plunk or splash, if it is the popping type. Lower the rod tip and gather in the slack line. Let the bug lie still again for fifteen or twenty seconds. Continue this jerk-pause retrieve until it is time to pick up and cast once more.

A bass may take the bug at any time, but most strikes come just as it starts to move after lying still. Set the hook by raising the rod sharply, meanwhile holding the line tightly with your left hand. Bass have hard mouths and it usually takes a sharp jerk to hook them.

TIP NO. 32

More Bass-Bugging Techniques

The slow, jerk-pause method of fishing a bass bug described in the previous tip no doubt catches more fish than any other, but occasionally another retrieve is more effective. If you don't catch bass with the jerk-pause method, try fishing your bug faster, with only a brief pause between jerks. Or, try pulling it slowly and steadily across the surface. Sometimes bass prefer a bug that doesn't make so much commotion. This is when the feather-minnow type bug with a bullet-shaped head pays off. And, not infrequently, a deer-hair bug works better than either the feather-minnow or popper.

Most of the time, where you fish a bug is more important than how you fish it. Along a rocky shore, drop the bug within inches of the rocks. Where brush overhangs the water, cast in under it as far as you can. Put your bug right on the edge of weeds or back into openings in the lily pads. You're not fishing right if you don't hang up occasionally. Many times bass simply won't come out for a bug that lands even a foot or two from cover.

Bug fishing is always better when the water is smooth. If the fishing slows down when the water gets choppy, switch to a bucktail and, if you still fail to catch fish, change to a fast-sinking line so that you can fish deeper.

In shallow lakes and ponds during hot weather there isn't much difference in water temperature from top to bottom. It may be too warm for comfort, which makes bass inactive, hugging the bottom, but they can't change their habitat completely as they do in deep lakes. Fish your bug along the shore, among the lily pads, and close to other cover in late evening, at night, and early in the morning when the water is coolest and the bass are most likely to be feeding. Your best chance during midday is to fish deep.

Catching bass on bugs at night is wonderfully exciting, and the darker it is the better. A full moon may be great for romance, but the bass don't like it. Sometimes a black fly fished deep will take them when the moon is on the water, but seldom a bug.

A popping bug is best at night and white is a good color. Color probably doesn't make any difference to the bass, but you can pick it up more easily with your flashlight when you cast into the weeds and brush. Don't use a flashlight any more then necessary — it frightens bass.

TIP NO. 33

Try the Deer-Hair Frog

The large-winged bass flies of yesteryear have almost been abandoned by today's flyrod bass and pike fishermen. Today the most popular flyrod bass lure is the cork-body popper. Yet a far more effective lure exists — the hair frog.

The hair frog, in all its variations, has a realistic action closely imitating that of a swimming frog, except that the gurgle and wake are more subdued. The hair frog's soft body allows the fish to grab hold easily, and hooking a fish is much easier than with cork poppers.

Unfortunately, the hair frog soaks up water. In ten casts it is so waterlogged that it swims under the surface. Spraying with silicone helps. Also, frogs that have the hair tightly packed and clipped close do a lot better.

The hair frog is easy to tie, even for a beginner — just tie on deer body hair as you would a muddler. Tie it on thick and tight, clip it to shape, leaving a flat-surfaced mouth. Tie on yellow bucktail legs or natural deer hair, then tie a few tight loops of thread on the legs where the knee joints should be. Put a few drops of lacquer on the joints and after it has dried a bit, bend the legs into shape. Let the joint dry some more and then bend again and lacquer again until the joint is at the right angle. Now let the joint dry and harden.

Tie a dozen or so of these frogs so that you can change them as they get wet.

TIP NO. 34

Bucktails for Bass

The standard way to fish a bucktail or streamer fly in still water is to make your cast and then wait for the line and fly to sink. It may take only a second or two in shallow water, but in deep water half a minute or more. Then pull in a foot or so of line, pause briefly, and pull again. Continue pulling and pausing until the fly is retrieved, ready for another cast. When fishing from a boat let the line fall to the floor as you retrieve it. When wading form the line into coils in your left hand.

As with a bug, it sometimes pays to fish a bucktail faster or slower than usual. Experiment with long pulls and short pulls, both slow and fast. When you hook a fish, stay with the retrieve that got it. If you get more, fine. If not, try something different. If you don't find any near the surface, fish deeper and deeper.

Bucktails work in the spring when the bass are inshore. They continue to catch fish when the water gets warmer and the fish leave the shallows. As this occurs, fish farther and farther from shore, working out along gently sloping rock or gravel points, along rocky reefs, and over gravel bottom at various depths down to twenty-five or thirty feet. You need a fast-sinking line for this so that you do not have to wait long for the line to settle down to fish level.

Unlike bug fishing, long casts do help when you're fishing a bucktail deep. The farther you retrieve the fly at the level of the fish, the more likely a fish is to see it.

Despite the delights of bug fishing during the spring and early summer, hot weather is the best time to make a big catch of big bass. Find a good school of them and you'll clean up.

Then mark the spot well. You'll probably catch bass there all summer long and again the next year.

If the bass don't move inshore in the fall, as happens on some lakes, the method just described is the key to catching them from the time they leave the shallows in the early summer until winter sets in. There are exceptions, of course.

In some lakes both largemouth and white bass school in mid-winter, far above the bottom and far from shore. This can lead to wildly exciting bug fishing, even in August, when they drive schools of baitfish to the surface and start sloshing at them like mad. By and large though, working out from shore, fishing deeper and deeper, is the most consistent way to catch bass during the summer and fall.

TIP NO. 35

Jigs Are Hard to Beat

Bottom-bumping with jigs was a highly successful fishing technique in our grandfathers' day; surprisingly, many anglers still know little about it. Because of the erratic retrieving motion used, the jig has been found effective on a great many species of freshwater game fish.

Varying the speed of the retrieve can make all the difference. A slow retrieve with an occasional flip of the rod tip will usually put the whammy on nearby walleyes. On the other hand, lake trout are interested in jigs lowered to the bottom and then rushed back to the boat with a hurried, pumping motion. Smallmouth bass like jigs which dart and dally around shoreline rocks and ledges, just like crawfish crawling from one lair to another. Stream trout will hit tiny jigs which rest on the bottom and occasionally dart into the current and drop back to rest. Panfish take tiny jigs fished very slowly like streamer flies.

Color is not as important in jigs as the action used, but it is important enough to spell the difference between success and failure on tough days. Smallmouth bass and walleyes like blue, yellow, and white, although walleyes sometimes prefer black. Largemouth bass and pike like black. Trout like orange, green, and brown. Panfish like white with pink heads.

Weights of jigs may vary from two ounces down to $1/32$ of an ounce. The very heavy jigs are used mainly for lake trout, where the heavy tackle fisherman wants to get into cold water lairs in a hurry. Bass jigs may run from a quarter to three-quarter ounces, also a good range for walleye. Stream trout and panfish prefer the 1/16 and $1/32$-ounce jigs which can be handled nicely on a flyrod or ultralight spinning tackle. Crappies fall easily for a jig retrieved about four feet under a bobber and jerked lightly.

The retrieve is all-important. Unless the angler supplies the action, there isn't any. Sometimes an even, low-speed jigging motion will do the job. Sometimes it takes a big heave-and-fall-back action to get results. Watch a genuine jig fisherman go about his work, then learn by continued practice and effort. There is still a lot to be learned about jig fishing and, who knows, you may come up with a great method.

Tricks with jigs include putting a little flavor on the hook when fish such as walleye are being coy. A piece of live nightcrawler or the tail section of a minnow often works magic, especially if fished very slowly among the rocks on the bottom. Or, jigs can be successfully trolled at slow speeds with an occasional flip of the rod tip for more action. A single spinner on the front of a jig is effective for northern pike and walleyes.

Jigs are a top producing lure for many different game fish. For walleyes, they're impossible to beat.

TIP NO. 36

How to Catch More Fish on Jigs

Unlike many artificial baits, leadhead jigs display little action of their own. A jig's appeal is determined by its appearance and by the method of working it. You can bounce or hop a jig, or swim it straight. Your retrieve can be fast or slow, near the surface, or along the bottom.

To help catch more fish in jig time, here are some tips:
- When casting for walleyes and bass, variations of the simple lift-and-drop retrieve often work best. While retrieving your jig, repeatedly pull your rod tip forward and let it back. This pumping motion of the rod allows the jig to hop along the bottom. Sometimes you'll catch more fish by exaggerating this action with sharp sweeping strokes of the rod; at other times you'll score with short twitches or even a straight retrieve.
- Use monofilament line with jigs, as light as conditions permit. A useful guideline: the smaller the jig, the lighter the line.
- For best results, tie your jig directly to the line. Avoid leaders, snaps, swivels, and sinkers. If more weight is needed — to cast against wind or to compensate for boat speed — go to a heavier jig.
- When dressing jigs with small minnows or pieces of worm, sock it to them right away, especially when fish are hitting hard. But with large minnows and whole nightcrawlers, point your rod tip toward the fish for a moment before setting the hook. The brief hesitation allows the fish time to work the bait and the hook into its mouth.
- Fish sometimes scoop jigs right off the bottom! When you've dressed the minnows, pork strips, plastic worms, or other

bait, you'll get more bottom bites with a Lindy Dingo. This jig literally stands on its head and elevates the hook; bait is readily seen and easy to grab.
- Slow trolling and drifting maintain your preferred jigging action without the usual casting and retrieving. How much line to let out depends on the depth of the fish, the weight of the jig, and the speed of the boat. Trolling and drifting methods are ideal for locating fish.
- Often fish hit jigs on the drop. An alert angler can detect these hard-to-notice strikes by watching the line closely for unusual behavior — for example, a telltale twitch or knock on the line. Sometimes the line moves off to one side or stops while the jig is settling. If you suspect a fish, set the hook immediately.

Regardless of how you do it with jigs, *you* provide the action. That's what makes jigging such a great sport!

TIP NO. 37

Windy Weather Lures

Every angler should have a few lures with heavy sectional density in his tackle box for windy weather. Wind can play havoc with lures — one cast goes there, the other goes yonder. Only heavy, compact lures can be cast with any semblance of accuracy.

In wind plugs are a poor bet. They are too light. Spinners with broad blades and big squirrel tails are also a poor choice, as are thin wide spoons with much surface area.

What you need are heavy, narrow spoons made of thick metal. Compact spinners with lead heads or bodies are another good bet. So are jigs. Make sure you have a few of each in your tackle box.

TIP NO. 38

Rigs for Bluegills

When the summer doldrums hit, bluegills, the big fat ones that taste so good straight from the frying pan, can be hard to catch, particularly in the midday hours. Then bluegills stay close to the bottom and perhaps even hide among the bottom weeds.

When this happens, tie on a foam-bodied stonefly nymph or a foam spider. Above the lure, pinch on a split-shot sinker. Where to pinch the sinker depends on the height of the underwater vegetation where you are fishing. At first, try a foot and, if the hook catches weeds, go higher. Then put on a slim bobber to signal even the tiniest nibble. If the rig is to work, the lure must float just above the reeds. Then cast out and retrieve slowly, working the lure a bit. You can, of course, also troll.

A similar rig can be used, but in this case omit the split-shot and use a small sinking plug. Attach the bobber so that the plug will just skim over the top of the weeds. Remember, the bobber must be slim so as not to cause much of a ripple when you reel in or troll.

Still another rig to use is a small weedless hook baited with garden worms. The "red wigglers" are really good for this. Put a small bobber (a cork is the best because of its neutral color) ahead of it, then a big sinker ahead of the bobber. The sinker must be heavy enough to sink the whole rig. The bobber will float up, taking the hook with it. The bobber should float above the weeds, with the hook floating among their tops. For best results, keep this rig moving by casting out and reeling in slowly, very slowly, or trolling. It's not a bad idea to brighten up the hook a bit with a tiny spinner just ahead of it.

TIP NO. 39

Secrets of Successful Crappie Fishing

I can guarantee successful crappie fishing: follow my method and you will catch these papermouths fifty-two weeks a year. Too good to be true? No! It works every time.

Finding crappie is usually the hardest job. Obviously, if you know where they live, it is easier. So, build them some homes. Start with at least five brush piles. I say five because two men can easily build five piles at varying depths in one day.

The first step: Tour your favorite crappie lake, using a depth finder to locate five spots with depths of approximately 22, 20, 18, 16, and 14 feet. Mark each spot with a buoy. These should be near creek channels or drop-offs, and the brush piles should be set near deep-water access. Crappie prefer brush near deep water so they can flee there if the weather changes or if they are frightened.

To build the brush pile, combine cedar and oak, tying two to five small trees together with a wire or heavy-duty staging using a heavy rock or a cement block as a weight. Load the brush on a boat or floating platform and tow it to the preselected site.

At the spot, dump the brush beside the buoy marker. Wait for five or ten minutes, then cruise over the area until the brush pile appears on the depth finder. As it flashes on your finder, select two on-shore reference points (Figure 1). You may think you can find the brush anytime, but different conditions will exist with each trip and it may well be impossible to find that brush pile. You'll save a lot of time by lining up reference points for every pile.

Repeat this process for all five crappie beds, wait a few

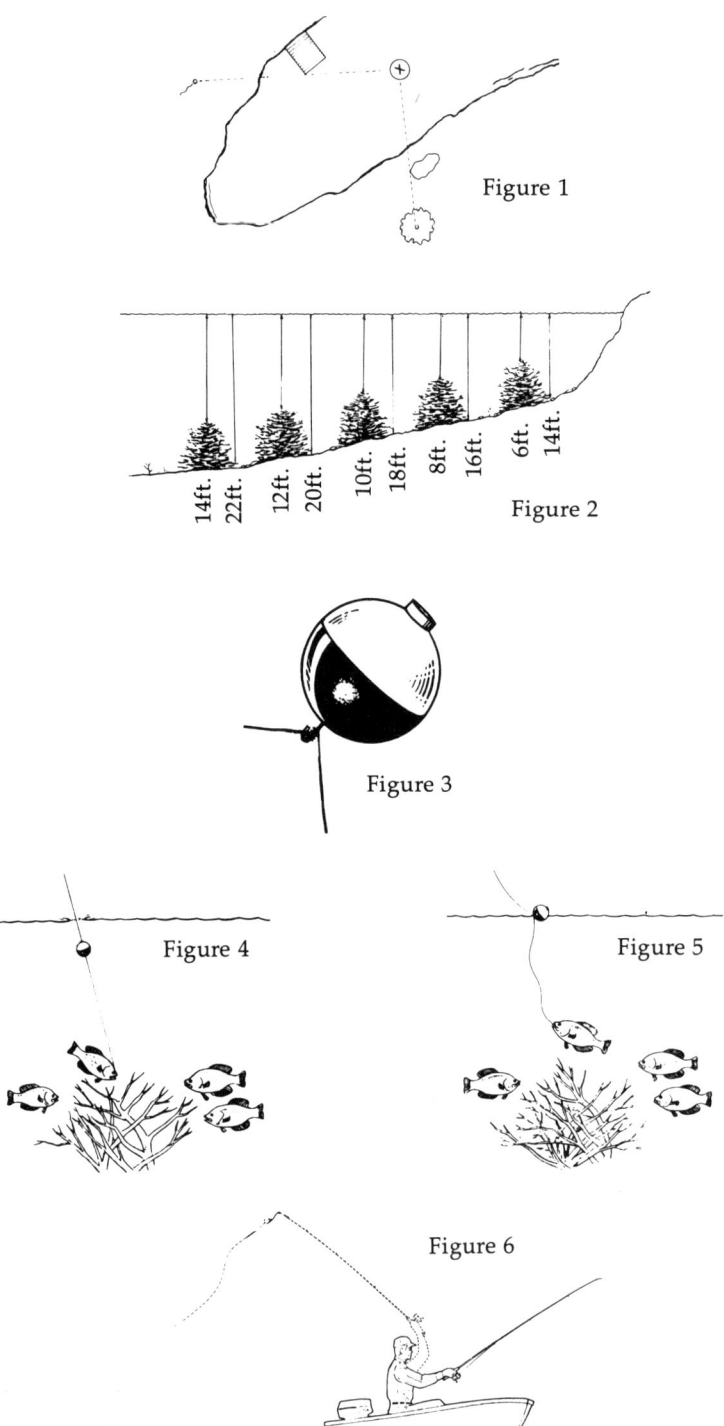

weeks, then start catching crappie. Note that the brush piles were set at 22, 20, 18, 16, and 14 feet. If the heights of the brush are seven or eight feet, the tops will come approximately 14, 12, 10, 8 and 6 feet from the surface (Figure 2).

Start fishing over the fourteen-foot brush pile with the tops six to seven feet deep. Locate the brush on the finder, drop a buoy marker, and anchor a comfortable casting length away. If the brush pile is seven feet from the surface, tie on a jig, measure approximately $6^{1}/_{2}$ feet up the line and attach a bubble cork by wrapping the line three or four times on the bottom portion of the cork only (Figure 3). When you cast near the buoy wait a few seconds; the weight of the jig will float the bubble cork in an upright position. (A yellow top with an orange bottom is my favorite one-inch cork because of its visibility in all conditions.)

Color is important because after the jib sinks, only the top is exposed. At this point, start bobbing the cork by twitching the rod tip, reeling in your crappie rig slowly. Watch for two things. While the cork bobs, the jig is doing the same thing, tantalizing the crappie to nail it. First, watch for the cork going under. That is the easiest hit to spot. It means the crappie are either at the same level as the jig or just over it and are taking the jig straight down (Figure 4). As soon as the cork disappears, gently set the hook.

The more common hit, especially in the fall and winter, comes if the crappie are under the jig and come up on it. As soon as a fish hits the jig, the line goes slack and, because the cork is tied only on the bottom, it will tip sideways and show the orange bottom (Figure 5). When you see this orange flash, set the hook.

Now, let's discuss the tight line method. The cork system works with tightly structured crappie because there's less chance of hanging in the brush and spooking the school. But when the crappie are scattered, the tight line works better. Simply work the entire area around your brush, letting the jig sink to the bottom and creep, or jig it, over the brush, keeping the line taut at all times, waiting until you feel what I call a tump, or hit.

When crappie are hitting, just fishing one hole will be all you can handle. But if for some reason you don't find the crappie in the first hole, go to the other brush piles.

One of the brush piles I recommended had a twenty-two foot lake bottom. If your brush comes to within fourteen feet of the surface, you may doubt you can set your cork at thirteen feet and cast properly. You can do it with a buggy-whip action, similar to a flyfisherman's (see Figure 6). It looks strange and takes some practice, but on an extremely cold day the crappie will be deep and the deep hole will be the producer. With five brush piles, you have a good start. Keep adding to the number of crappie beds at every opportunity. Build several brush piles at the same level because when they're hitting in a pile seven feet from the surface, they probably will be active in similar piles.

By the way, you do not have to fish just the brush piles you build. Find the beds other people build and fish them too. Renowned crappie fisherman and tackle manufacturer Cotton Cordell said to me one day, "They're just as good as the ones you build, only you didn't have to do the work." But you must not get upset when someone finds and fishes in one of your brush piles.

I use a graphite rod (because I am convinced that you can feel a crappie hit better with graphite than with glass) and a good quality spinning reel. A white chicken feather jig has been my best producer, outfishing everything else five to one.

Check your local game and fish agency as to the legality of building brush piles and, if you get the green light, build on. You will soon get a reputation as a great crappie catcher and you'll make a bunch of new friends at the dinner table. The Good Lord could have made a better-tasting fish than a crappie, but he didn't need to.

TIP NO. 40

Give Carp a Try

I've always felt carp to be the fish of the future. Why? Because it will live and prosper in waters too polluted for any other fish. This may be a sad reflection of the way we have mistreated our waters, but it is true. Our waters are still being polluted faster than they are being cleaned up, despite a greater than ever concern about our environment. Until this trend is reversed, carp are the fish of the future, particularly for the ordinary Joe Angler who can't afford to fly to Labrador or some other as yet unpolluted fisherman's Utopia.

The carp is a challenging fish to catch, more challenging than many more highly sought-after species. It may be homely, but it is not dumb. It is a big fish and a strong fighter; wary by nature and with a delicate mouth. Indeed, for its size, the mouth is very small.

No fancy equipment is needed except a stout rod to set the hook. The rod should be fairly long for good leverage. The reel should be a good size and have a good smooth drag. (Carp can go on runs that would do credit to a steelhead.) The line should be monofilament; twelve pounds is good, but a lighter line is even better, if you can handle it. The hooks should be strong and not too large. A No. 5 is a good choice, but my preference goes to the No. 10 treble hook because it holds dough balls better.

Rig your lure with a sliding sinker. Never use a fixed sinker. If a carp feels resistance or weight as it picks up your bait, most of the time he will drop it. Lighter lines are better because they offer less resistance. Spinning or spin-casting reels are better than a casting reel for the same reason — the line just slips off the fixed spool.

Carp will eat just about anything. A buddy once caught one on a plug lying on the bottom because of a backlash. Any of the smelly concoctions used for catfish are also good carp bait. Gum drop candy and niblets of corn are two effective and easily obtained baits. But the most popular carp bait is dough balls. If I had a ten-dollar bill for every dough ball recipe, I could go on a tiger fish safari on the upper Nile or after golden bass in the headwaters of the Amazon. Just about every ingredient to hold the dough balls together has been used, from sassafras to wine to cotton shreds. Here is my favorite. (I wouldn't let you slip away without telling you about it.)

A carp locates its food primarily through its sharp sense of smell, located in its barbels or whiskers. And what smells better than Aunt Agatha's vanilla cookies? Nothing, and that's my secret.

Pour a bottle of vanilla into a mixing bowl and add bran or wheat flakes. Knead this until you have a gooey ball of dough. Stick it in an airtight plastic container and hide it in the refrigerator. Yes, hide it. The concoction is quite tasty; it attracts both kids and carp.

When you bait your hook, use a fairly small dough ball. You want the carp to swallow it whole, not just nibble — otherwise you won't hook it. Remember, a carp has a small mouth.

After your cast is made and the bait has settled to the bottom, keep your line slack. Carefully watch the line where it enters the water. Any slight movement indicates a bite.

The much scorned carp is a challenging fish to catch — a fish that comes much harder than a number of highly sought game fish. Here, Dan Gapen, the lure manufacturer, proudly holds up a big carp caught on one of his Ugly Bugs.

TIP NO. 41

Separating the Pike-Perches

The fine-tasting walleye and its cousin, the sauger, are both pike-perches. As with many families, there is a strong resemblance, so strong that at times they are hard to distinguish.

Most fishermen identify them by general appearance. The sauger is a more slender and smaller fish than walleye. Also, at times, it has mottled sides as opposed to the greengold or walleye. But these characteristics can be deceiving, so here are two foolproof ways of identifying the pike-perches:

Sauger — the spiny dorsal fin is speckled, while the pectoral fin near the gill cover has a black or gray blotch.

Walleye — the spiny dorsal fin is not speckled, but has a black blotch at the base, while the pectoral fin is clear gray or brown with no blotch.

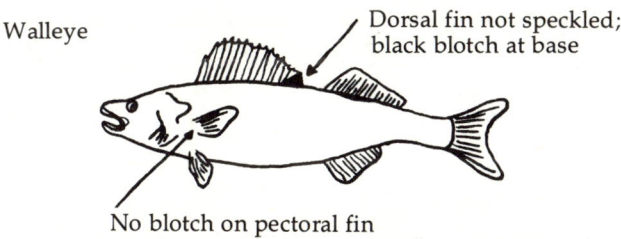

Walleye — Dorsal fin not speckled; black blotch at base

No blotch on pectoral fin

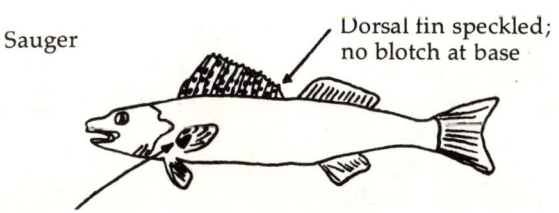

Sauger — Dorsal fin speckled; no blotch at base

Black or gray blotch on pectoral fin

TIP NO. 42

For Summer Walleyes, Keep Moving Deep and Slow

Nobody can really call the walleye a great game fish. It is simply not a spectacular battler. But it is voracious and, like a bulldog, tenacious. It grabs and hangs on. This doesn't mean that a walleye isn't fun to catch — it is. And, on light tackle, it can be quite exciting.

The best thing about a walleye is its taste. In my books, juicy walleye fillets fresh from lake to skillet are unbeatable. Another walleye plus is that it lives in pretty waters; picturesque rocky lakes and clean, relatively fast streams and rivers.

The only problem is catching them. The fish is voracious and not very wary, but not all fishermen find walleye easy to catch. There are two reasons for this: first, walleyes, because they are greedy, predatory fish, are almost consistently on the move looking for prey. Since they are also a school fish, it doesn't take them long to deplete a pocket of minnows or crawfish and move on. Second, during the daylight hours, they cruise and hunt close to the bottom.

Neither obstacle is insurmountable. First, fish the most likely spots. In lakes, this means close to rocky bars and islands, particularly near sudden drop-offs. Another good spot is where a stream runs into a lake. In rivers the fish can usually be caught below swift runs, in eddy water, and below dams. Second, keep moving and exploring until you find the first walleye. Then concentrate on that spot. Unless the walleye is a stray, it is one of a school. Catching the first one is the hard part.

A stringer of summer walleyes like this one comes only by fishing deep and slow.

Third, fish deep. The walleye is not known for its speed, so you must also fish slowly. Deep running and bottom-bumping plugs are good lures. Dark colors are best. The jig is another good lure — and one of the most versatile, particularly for casting. But in my book, the best walleye lure is the old June bug spinner, with its big, long-shanked hook baited with a fat night crawler, a good-sized minnow, or a crawfish. Today walleye fishermen rarely use the June bug. Why I don't know; maybe we have become too gadget conscious. We are too easily taken in by new lures and tend to ignore the old, inexpensive ones. This is a mistake because a lure has not been invented that can beat the June bug in walleye water.

TIP NO. 43

For Walleyes Try Some Moonshine

Many fishermen know that the best fishing for walleyes is at night. The walleye's large whitish pupil works best in subdued light. This is why walleyes in the bright, midday hours tend to stick to deep water: the bigger the fish the deeper the water. But what many walleye fishermen don't know is that some of the best walleye fishing is when moonlight is at its brightest at full moon.

Why? Because on the bright nights that accompany a full moon, crawfish are most active. They crawl out from under rocks and from crevices to feed on bits of carrion, insects, and the like. Walleyes know this, and take full opportunity of the fine feast offered them by moonlight. The thing to remember is that crawfish are most numerous in shallow water, in gravel, and on rocky bars. This is where you should be doing your moonshine walleye fishing. Crawfish of course are good bait, but so are dull-colored jigs and bottom-bumping plugs.

A warning. Keep quiet in your boat, and don't stomp or splash around on shore. In shallow water walleyes spook easily.

TIP NO. 44

Don't Neglect Gravel Bars

Gravel bars are submerged mounds of sand and gravel at varying depths, usually the hatching area for various insects and the home of crawfish and game fish fry. In shallow water the bars are feeding areas; in deep water they are loafing areas. Best results in the shallows are obtained by casting over the bar and bringing the lure up over the top and down the other side. In deep water, anglers score well by trolling the length of the bar with deep-running spoons and plugs.

TIP NO. 45

Separating the Pikes

Many anglers don't realize that the northern pike, the muskie and the chain pickerel are all pikes. They all belong to the genus *Esox: Esox lucius*, the northern pike; *Esox masquinongy*, the muskellunge; and *Esox niger*, the chain pickerel.

Most anglers use color and pigmentation to tell these fish apart. Yet color is the least reliable technique. It varies from lake to lake and from one geographic race of fish to another. Young fish in particular can be difficult to distinguish. Think of the embarrassment of an angler whose northern turns out to be a young muskie when checked by a conservation officer. But the real dilemma comes a moment later when the conservation officer confiscates the fish and the tackle. Why? Because many states and provinces have a minimum size limit (usually twenty-six to thirty inches) on muskies. A piece of fiction? No, I've seen several anglers caught this way.

Here is a foolproof way to identify the pikes:

Muskie — no scale on lower half of gill cover or cheek.

Northern pike — cheek is fully scaled and lower gill cover has no scale.

Pickerel — both the gill cover and the cheek are fully scaled.

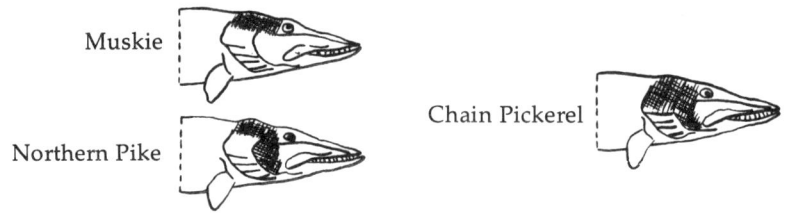

TIP NO. 46

Fishing for Old Sharptooth

The sharptooth, because of a nasty disposition which makes it a tough scrapper, is often classified as the meanest fish that swims. Fisheries biologists claim that it does not have to be hungry to attack an angler's lure. It enjoys ripping into a lure and delights in exploding the water's surface into a frothy bomb of fish and water.

The pike's narrow form can be seen lurking shadowy still in the weed beds. When it wants a bait, you can see it coming.

Like a torpedo it gains speed. At the last moment awesome jaws open wide and the bait is devoured. Few baitfish or lures escape the needlelike teeth. It clamps down hard and shakes its massive head, earning its reputation as a mean, tackle-testing torpedo of the northern weed beds.

The northern is not a snobbish fish. When it comes to hitting baits, it is much less finicky than the muskie. From early June through September, the pike provides fast summer action in the northern lakes of the United States and through a good portion of Canada. Pike are also taken through the ice in the winter.

Serious pike anglers favor medium to heavy spinning and baitcasting outfits equipped with mono line in the ten to twenty-pound range. Twenty-pound northerns are common in many lakes and with this tackle the angler is ready for them as pike are found in the shallows in weeds and snags. Sometimes a big fish must be stopped before it gets into the brush.

Casting for northerns from a boat or shore tests accuracy rather than ability to cast great distances. Northerns are found in the shallows. The closer a fisherman can put a plug to weeds, lily pads, logs, or brush, the better are his chances of a strike. If a fisherman has developed a certain degree of accuracy, casting from a boat for pike doesn't present much of a problem. Casting from shore, however, may involve overcoming obstacles. The best pike spots are the patches of water with cover, both in the water and on shore. Overhanging trees provide shade for pike during the heat of the day, but presenting a bait to a pike from a tangled shoreline can be rough.

If an angler does not have access to a boat on a pike lake, his success can be almost as high as the boater's by using waders and getting past many of the snags to give himself room to cast. Hip waders are good; chest waders even better. In many instances, prime pike water is not very deep. You can wade close enough to cover it with long casts. Again, a rod with enough muscle to keep pike out of the snags is recommended.

There is really no best bet for pike lures. In the morning

bucktails with silver blades and red and white feathers are especially good. Floating silver minnows, about four inches long, are well suited to weedy shallows. Spinners and spoons generally become bogged down with weeds, but light minnows can be virtually weedless. Spoons work well in deeper water near gravel bars. A red and white combination, along with silver, sometimes brings pike to the net. Yellow and white lead-headed jigs are good for both pike and walleye. Fished among the snags, they are potent, but easily hung up.

The pike's sharp teeth can put a quick end to the contest between man and fish. It is wise to check lines often for signs of fraying. Wire leaders, with snap swivels attached, may be awkward at times, but they can mean the difference between landing that trophy pike and losing a favorite lure.

TIP NO. 47

Psyching a Pike

The pike is one of nature's most efficient predators. It is perfectly evolved for its life-style. I think of the pike as the leopard of fresh water. Like the leopard, it is perfectly camouflaged, lean and strong, and deadly. When a hungry pike stalks a fish, it means business.

When pike are hungry, they will strike at almost anything; the small, stunted, ever-hungry pike in the small northern lakes are good examples of this. But the big northerns on big waters are a different breed of cat. Like all predators, when they have a full belly, they are finicky, and that's the time when you must know how to psych them if you want results.

There is one thing a pike can't resist, even with a full belly: a

There is one thing a pike can't resist, even with a full belly, and that's a crippled minnow or a lure that is fished like one.

crippled minnow moving close to its lair. The pike's predatory nature just won't allow the crippled minnow to pass by. So capitalize on it — present your lures like wounded baitfish.

Here are my favorite techniques: On a cloudy day or in the evening at dusk when the water is mirror still, I use silver-colored surface lures that swim with their heads submerged but their tails above water. These lures create only a soft "V" on the surface. The real trick is in moving the rod tip from side to side in a 90-degree arc to make the lure zigzag. Small fish in their death throes swim this way — erratically on the surface.

This trick won't work in windy weather because waves will obscure the soft movement of the lure. It also doesn't work well at night, mainly I think because the lure is hard to see.

In breezy weather or when rain dimples the lake's surface, I switch to surface lures that have two small spinners on both ends. I work these lures at a moderate speed so that the spinner blades cut a V-shaped wake through the waves. Again the zigzag motion is a must. This lure also works better in the dark because it makes a bit of noise to attract the pike. Neither of these lures are effective during bright daylight. This, again, I think is because the pike may see your boat as it follows the lure. Remember, when a northern is not hungry, it follows a crippled baitfish more slowly and will not strike as viciously. Because of the slower speed, its chances of seeing you and your boat are better.

During the daylight hours, I use sinking lures, preferably spoons — either in bright silver, perch-colored, or the old red-and-white. Again, I try to give the spoon erratic movements. I zigzag the spoon back and forth, but I also add a downward flutter. I reel the lure in a couple of feet with my rod tip high; then quickly lower the rod tip and let the spoon flutter to the bottom. If the bottom is a fair way down, I strip some line off my drag.

In fishing weedy waters you may have to use weedless spoons, but there are a couple of other possibilities. I use a floating, minnow-like plug that submerges on being retrieved.

I then work the plug in a zigzag motion at a speed just fast enough for the plug to swim over the weed tops but not into them. Every few feet I stop reeling and let the plug float up to the surface. On the surface I give it a few twitches and take it down again.

The other trick for weedbeds is to rig a good-sized bucktail spinner or a spoon with a bobber above the spinner and a sinker above the bobber. The rig should sink with the sinker on the bottom while the bobber is suspended part way up, bringing the lure up above the weeds. The rig is now cast out and retrieved in a zigzag, springing and starting through weedbeds.

The best pike-getting trick of all is to use a baitfish — a big one. A ten-inch sucker is my favorite. I hobble the sucker with a good sinker. Hook the sucker through both lips with a big, forged hook with a turned-out point. Now, cast out with it or troll slowly — very slowly, stopping periodically. The sinker should drag on the bottom with the sucker swimming above it. To a pike, this will look like a wounded fish.

A sucker fished this way is the deadliest lure of all. Even in heavily fished waters where pike have become hardware-shy, this trick will work. When a fish strikes, give it lots of slack line so it can swim away with its prey and enough time so it can turn the sucker and swallow it. (Pike always swallow big baitfish headfirst.)

TIP NO. 48

How to Fish Weedbeds

Pike, bass, and muskie often feed in weedbeds. Here's how to get them out and on to your stringer: Position your boat quietly about forty feet from the bed. Using a weedless lure, cast into the vegetation. Use a slow retrieve, with short pauses, and work the lure through the growth. At the bed's end there is usually a drop-off. When the lure reaches this point, let it sink to the bottom. Pause. Now retrieve, as fast as possible. If there's a fish in the area, he'll clobber the lure during that last retrieve.

TIP NO. 49

To Catch a Muskie

There is only one universally accepted formula for catching muskies — you have to know where they are. It helps even more if you know where a specific muskie lies.

Lacking this information, your best bet is to go out with a muskie guide or a successful muskie fisherman. Then you'll learn what kind of water muskies prefer, how deep they lie, and under what conditions one is likely to make a lunge at your bait.

Where do muskies live in muskie water? In the shallow bays and around sand bars with emergent vegetation in mid-lake. That's where the food is. If you ever get a rise or even a surface boil from a muskie, mark the spot well and come back another day. One lives there.

Each muskie, so say biologists, requires its own territory, roughly about a hundred feet square, to live and feed, and it drives out all competitors from this area. Learn where one lives and keep at it with big baitcasting plugs. Sooner or later you'll get a take. It takes years of experience to know where each muskie lies and when it is most likely to hit. Even that won't always serve you in good stead, for here's a fish that is the most tantalizing, perverse, crotchety, temperamental, and unfathomable critter that swims.

The muskie is the most tantalizing, perverse, crotchety, temperamental, and unfathomable fish that swims. To catch one, an angler must have infinite patience and a tireless casting arm.

Erratic in behavior and contemptuous in attitudes, muskies are also unpredictable and eccentric in their tastes in lures. On some days they prefer plugs. On other days they will take only red-and-white spoons. Some days yellow bucktails with spinners do business. Other times only brown or black bucktails with spinners. Then there will be catches on a flashing silver spoon, which theoretically imitates a whitefish, but on any given day these spoons may produce nothing.

Underwater or surface plugs? It depends on the weather. If there's a ripple on the water, or white-capped waves, go under with deep-riding plugs. If the water is calm and flat, stay on top. Retrieves should vary with every cast — fast one time, fast and halting the next time, slow another time, then slow and halting.

The best time of the summer for muskie fishing seems to be when the weather is hottest and the forage fish that muskies feed on (perch and whitefish) have retreated to the cool depths. Muskies don't follow them by choice, but lie in their shallow lairs waiting for anything that comes by on top.

But, above all, muskie fishing requires infinite patience and a tireless arm. You have to work to catch a muskie.

TIP NO. 50

Separating the Salmonids

With the recent addition of coho and chinook salmon to the fish of the Great Lakes, thousands of anglers are faced with identifying these two from the other salmonid, the steelhead. Proper identification is a must. Some states have different limits on each, and the fisherman who cannot accurately identify the fish he is catching isn't much of an angler.

Coho (silver salmon) — gray mouth; white or light gray gums; forked tail, spots on upper half only; anal fin has twelve to fifteen rays.

Chinook — black mouth and gums; serrated tail, spots on all of tail; anal fin has fifteen to nineteen rays.

Steelhead (rainbow or Kamloops trout) — white mouth and gums; square tail, spots on all of tail; anal fin has eleven rays or less.

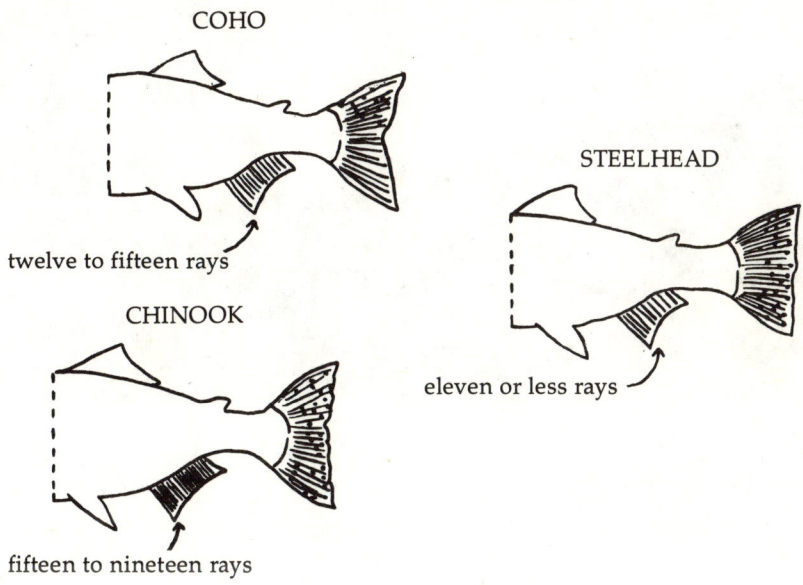

TIP NO. 51

Steelheading Is a Matter of Feel

Choosing the right rod is key. The strike of a steelhead can be as soft as if your lure had hung up for a moment on the bottom, but once you get one of these sleek battlers to bite, you need

To catch steelhead like these, you have to develop "feel" — to know exactly what your lure or bait is doing out there in the water at all times.

enough muscle in the rod to drive the hook home into a tough jaw. You need a rod with a sensitive tip to feel those bites, yet you need strength to set the hook and to do battle once you get it on.

At other times a steelhead can grab your lure and start running as if it were going to take all of your line with it. This hard strike often comes when using bobbers, spoons, or other artificial lures. In this case, your rod needs enough backbone for either the angler or the fish to set the hook if the fish takes off on the run.

Some anglers set the hook, reel in several turns, and then sock it to the fish again. They would rather get a solid hook or lose the fish right at the start than have a lightly hooked fish come off after the battle has been going on for some time.

But the rod is only part of the story. Once a fish has been hooked, the drag on your reel has to be smooth. If it hangs up, lets go, or is jerky, it can mean a lost fish from a broken line or leader. A steelhead battle is tough, with sudden turns, leaps, and runs.

Fishing gear helps in what steelheaders call feel. An expert knows what his lure or bait is doing out there on the bottom at all times. He can even watch a novice at work and know when there is a bite before the beginner knows it. One of these old pros can work a gob of eggs through a drift several times without hanging up. A novice on that same stretch of water may hang up half the time.

A veteran steelheader knows when a fish picks up his eggs. The beginner may not realize it until he reels in and sees the smashed eggs.

This matter of feel is most important in steelheading. The expert has a sixth sense that lets him raise his rod gently over rocks and snags that reach out and grab the gear of others. Yet the expert keeps his gear down on the bottom where the fish are.

TIP NO. 52

Lure-Drifting for River Rainbows

Lure-drifting is a fishing technique used by top anglers and fishing guides for steelhead and salmon in the fast-flowing rivers of the West Coast. It works equally well on rainbows and coho in Eastern rivers. The best lures submerge and dig down to six feet of water using only the pressure of the current; the Flatfish and Tadpoly are the most popular.

You will need a rod with a sensitive tip, but with enough backbone in the butt section to handle sixty or seventy feet of twelve to fifteen-pound test line.

Start the lure drifting above a good holding water with the boat headed upstream, running your motor just fast enough to lose ground and drift slowly downstream. Let out about sixty feet of line. The current going by the lure will give it the action. The boat should be slowly zigzagged back and forth across the holding water so that the lure has a chance to thoroughly cover the area. The trick is to learn how fast to let the boat drift so that the lure has good action and goes down deep. Experience is the best teacher. After an afternoon or two on the water, you'll be able to gauge whether you are drifting at the proper speed by the vibration of the lure on your rod tip.

Since the only suitable lures are those which dig down by themselves in the face of a current, you'll find that the lures will drift around boulders and rocks and swing into eddies behind these obstacles, the places where rainbows lie. If your lure gets snagged, don't put tension on to try to free it. Give it plenty of slack and in most cases the lure will float free. This can't be done with weighted lures.

Lure-drifting has the tremendous advantage of working down over the fish. It also lets you cover more water than you could cover from shore. The technique is perfect for tyro anglers who can't cast properly — it will produce fish for them when no other method will.

In small streams this same technique can be used when wading. Use a long rod and wade out into the stream above the holding water. Face directly downstream, pointing your rod at arm's length to the nearest shore and letting out thirty or forty feet of line. Now, slowly make a 180-degree swing — a semicircle — with your rod so that it points to the opposite shore. Let out another two feet of line and swing your rod back to the original shoreline. Continue swinging the rod back and forth, at the same time letting out a bit more line with each pass, until the lure has covered all of the holding water.

TIP NO. 53

Drift Rig for Bottom Steelheads

If you fish for steelhead with a spinning outfit in waters loaded with sinker-snagging boulders, here is a fine rig you may want to try. It works equally well with worms, egg clusters, and flies. Tie a two-foot leader to a swivel. Crimp and then attach your hook. Between the split-shot and the swivel, put on a pencil sinker, twisting it on with a single twist to the leader. Use a single twist so that when the sinker gets caught it will twist free from the leader.

The weight of the pencil sinker is, of course, determined by the weight of your line and rod, the speed of the current, and the distance you need to cast. With this rig, you need never fear that the leader will tangle. It drifts out in the current. When using flies, make the leader a long one — about five feet.

TIP NO. 54

Nymph Fishing the Easy Way

Every trout stream has water that is seldom fished, even by experienced anglers. The placid pools and quiet holding waters are easy to spot, but pockets behind rocks, turbulent water ahead of pools, and riffles where feeder streams enter are frequently overlooked.

These spots are perfect for small nymphs, but your imitations must be realistic. The best way to assure this is to collect samples of live nymphs from the stream bed or from the stomach of caught trout. Use these as a pattern. Fortunately, the caddis fly larva is the bread and butter nymph of many trout streams. The caddis is easier to imitate realistically than the stonefly or mayfly nymphs. Keep your imitations small. Sizes 12 or 14 and even a few 16's are more productive than the larger sizes. To be well outfitted, you should have half a dozen nymphs of each size in all the common patterns.

The leader for fast-water fishing should be at least nine feet long, terminating with a two-foot tippet no heavier than three-pound test — 5X. Since you will be fishing fast but shallow water, you will need either a weighted nymph or a weight on the leader. In shallow water, the weighted leader works better than weighted nymphs. Put a weight on the leader with a two to three-inch piece of .020-inch lead wire. The rod should be on the soft side and about eight feet long. Any floating line is suitable.

The technique is quite simple. No casting is done. With only about eight feet of line plus leader, you drop your nymph slightly upstream and directly cross current from all likely holding water with a simple arm wave. Let the nymph drift with the current. An occasional snag on moss or rocks shows that you are deep enough to produce trout. You can expect a strike any time during the free drift.

Persistence pays off even in simplified nymphing. Two dozen drifts per pocket or run are not too many if not every lie has been covered. A trout may let the imitation go by thirty-three times before taking it on the thirty-fourth presentation.

TIP NO. 55

Fishing Dry Flies

Fly fishing with dry flies is one of the great piscatorial delights. Yet many anglers deny themselves this pleasure because they believe it is an art wrapped in magic. A fly rod may be a magic wand, but that's only because it has the ability to restore tranquility in a man's soul after a week at work. But enough of philosophy, back to fishing dry flies.

Catching fish with dry flies can be difficult, but frequently it isn't. Begin by fishing only for trout that are rising. When trout are not feeding at the surface, forget about fishing them in this way. Concentrate your early efforts on fish that actually show themselves in rippling current. Don't concern yourself too much with your tackle. Any floating line is fine. Use a two-foot tippet of about four pounds on your leader. At this stage don't worry about fly patterns. When you see a trout rise, try casting a gray-colored fly above the spot and letting the fly float over the trout. Once the fish takes it, you are a dry fly fisherman. Everything you do after this will be a refinement. The tapered line, the long leader, and a lighter rod with faster action will all come later, as will the mystery and mastery of fly patterns. You are now well hooked on fishing with dry flies and it's an addiction from which you'll never be free.

TIP NO. 56

The Marabou Magic

Streamer fishing is a fine art. I state this positively because a special fishing buddy of mine is one of the artists, and what he does to us on a stream shouldn't happen to a dog.

Our favorite small river is good dry fly water, so we always start dry. But of course there are times when high water conditions and/or a complete absence of any visible surface activity begin to frustrate us. I am likely to go nymph; he invariably goes streamer.

He is a generous guy so he soon hails me, "Hey, fellow, come down here a minute."

I ought to know better but I always do.

"Just got a follow from a big one... from right across there in front of that ledge. Here, put on this streamer and take him."

So I tie on the proffered streamer and for the next twenty minutes conscienciously move it past the face of the ledge. Absolutely nothing.

"Guess I'll work on down," I say finally, clip off the streamer, return it and move away, fiddling in my tackle box for a familiar nymph.

So the guy ties on the streamer I've just returned to him. Makes one cast across to the ledge. Whammo, a sixteen-inch brown. See what I mean? Shouldn't happen to a dog.

And it doesn't happen quite as often lately because I've found what seems to be his secret weapon. It became painfully obvious that the difference between my buddy's streamer fishing and mine was the action he imparted to his fly. Fishing exactly the same water with the same fly, he took them and I didn't. I could see, of course, that with rod tip and hand twist he really swims his streamer, doesn't just heave it out and let it swing around in an arc. I could see him doing it, but I couldn't seem to bring it off.

If a streamer looks dead, who will want to eat it? Or, almost as bad, if it looks alive, fast-moving, healthy, and hard to catch, only the occasional blooming athlete will go for it. So, if I couldn't learn to give the proper action to my lure, how about getting a lure that had some proper action of its own? "Breathing" marabou was supposed to have some pathetic pulsations, especially when moved erratically and slowly like a cripple — a live cripple.

Marabou was supposed to have it. What's more, it does. For the past two seasons I have really come down hard on the marabous. I had always carried a couple in my streamer book but now I carry five patterns (in several sizes) and I use them. For trout *and* for bass. I'm completely sold on what they can do.

Admittedly, the aforementioned river where a lot of our trouting is done is not easy streamer water. The fast runs tend to hold smaller fish, while the old fellows hold in the big, rather still pools. You can fish a stiffish Light Spruce or Grizzly King or Gray Ghost around in a tumbling rapids all right. But when it comes to simulating a live but crippled baitfish in quiet water, marabou is the word. This is why a marabou streamer is right for bass in a pond too. Little moves of your line make it pulsate. It looks deceptively alive even when your fish can take a long hard look at it.

The five patterns I carry are White Marabou Muddler, Brown and White Marabou, Black Marabou, Gray and White Marabou, White Marabou. I carry these in Size 10 for delicate work and Size 6 to offer a mouthful. You can buy them or tie them, either weighted or unweighted. Orvis has them.

A weighted crippled minnow on a sinking flyline, struggling feebly along right down on the bottom, is a tempting object for the biggest trout. But I have an aversion to a weighted fly — some vague sense that I'm not getting the same natural action. So I usually struggle to work an unweighted pattern well down just with the sinking line and fairly short leader. I can't justify this prejudice against weighted patterns with any catch statistics, and it is true that a streamer struggling feebly along close down on the bottom is much more effective than the same streamer wafting around at mid-depth.

Anyway, whether you chose the weighted or unweighted, get yourself a few marabou streamers. Then use them — imaginatively. Work one slowly close to you to watch exactly what happens to those feathers as the fly moves in short pulls through the water. Get the feel of the lure. It has a personality and aliveness that you can see. Then cast it out and let it sink into quiet water or let it wash down into the likely backwash of a big boulder. I promise the results will convince you, as they have me, that marabou is magic on any trout or bass water.

TIP NO. 57

Unbeatable Bass Bait

No artificial lure has had a greater impact on largemouth bass fishing than the plastic worm. Bass fishermen use the worm more often than any other lure. This doesn't mean that spinners, top water plugs, and jigs are not as good. They are — sometimes. But day after day, more bass are caught with "the worm." If you need proof, look at the results of bass tournaments.

There are many techniques for fishing the worm, but one method stands out as the most accepted throughout the South where worm fishing is most widely practiced.

Let's say our cover is a rocky point with deep water on both sides. If there is no wind, approach the point quietly and cast parallel to the point, close to shore. Make successive casts progressively deeper. Let the worm sink until your line goes slack. Lower your rod tip, reel all slack out of your line to give you a feel of the worm and sinker, and just picture that worm crawling slowly over the bottom as you raise your rod tip toward a vertical position.

Be alert at all times because a bass frequently picks up the worm as it sinks, so maintain a fairly tight line to give you a continuous feel. Often this feel is nothing more than a slight sideways jump of your line or a slack as a bass picks up the worm and swims toward you. At other times you'll feel a single or multiple tug at the end of your line as a bass picks up the worm.

When you think that a bass has taken the worm, there is one cardinal rule to keep in mind — get the slack out of your line.

Day in and day out, more largemouth bass are caught on plastic worms than on any other lure.

You do this by quickly reeling the line and lowering your rod tip so as not to move the worm. Point the rod tip toward the bass, tighten the line just enough to check for a feel of the fish at the end, and set the hook. Set it hard! Hard means try to break both your line and rod tip. You can't, of course, but that's how much muscle it takes. The reason for this is that you have got to drive that hook through a gob of worm before you can set it in the bass's jaw. This is when most big bass, which have tougher jaws, are lost: lost because the fisherman sets the hook too gently, too casually, too inadequately.

The more you fish a plastic worm, the more you'll learn to feel it over bottom cover and know what it is doing. There is no substitute for hours behind a rod, so get out and fish as often as you can.

Here are some little things that make a big difference:

Snagged worms — when your worm hangs up on bottom cover, don't yank. Give it slack line and then gently twitch it with upward flicks of your rod tip. The sliding sinker or jig head will usually jump the worm loose. Watch it, though. This is the time when a big bass sometimes inhales it.

Change worms — when a worm becomes badly torn it will not act normally, so change it. If a bottom-going worm isn't doing business for you, try a floating worm back in weeds or lily pads. Don't be afraid to change.

Worm colors — the best judge of the best color to use is the bass. Start with purple. That's the most popular. After twenty-five casts try blue, black, natural, and so on. Find the one the bass want and stay with it until it cools. Keep probing for the one they want like a kid looking over a candy selection.

Watch your line — the first couple of end feet get a lot of abrasion as your line is dragged over cover, pounded by

The closer a fisherman can cast his plug to weeds, lily pads, logs, or other northern pike lairs, the better are his chances of catching northerns like these.

constant casting, and jerked against brush or tree limbs. So keep your line fresh by breaking off about two feet a couple of times a day.

The most common reasons for missing fish are: (1) you are striking too soon; (2) you are waiting too long; (3) you aren't striking the fish hard enough; (4) that's life and fishing. You can't hook one every time.

TIP NO. 58

Rigging the Plastic Worm

Here is how to rig the plastic worm for weedless fishing and for the best action.

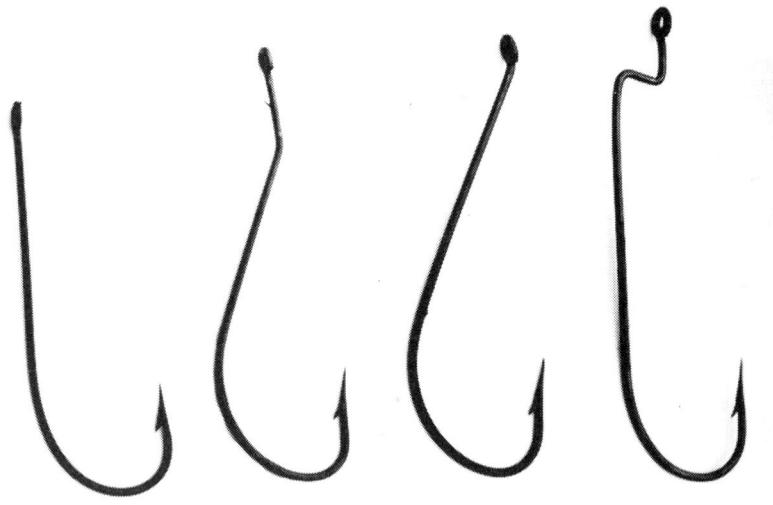

1. Hook types and sizes. Specialized hooks have been developed for plastic worm fishing. The bends or shank barbs help to hold the worm in position. Better hooking action is also claimed. Hook sizes can vary from 3/0 to 7/0, depending on the fisherman, but be sure they are strong.

2. Slide sinker system. Components:
a. Bullet-type slide sinker ($1/4$ to $1/2$ ounce)
b. Extra-strong worm hook (3/0 to 7/0)
c. Plastic worm
Thread mono through slide sinker and tie on hook.

3. Thread worm on hook. Start point of hook in center of the worm head and at about a thirty-degree angle; force the hook point outside the worm.

4. Completed slide sinker worm rig.

TIP NO. 59

The Knot for Plastic Worms

The knot on the plastic worm hook has to be stong and firm. It must not impair the action of the worm. The Burknot is the best.

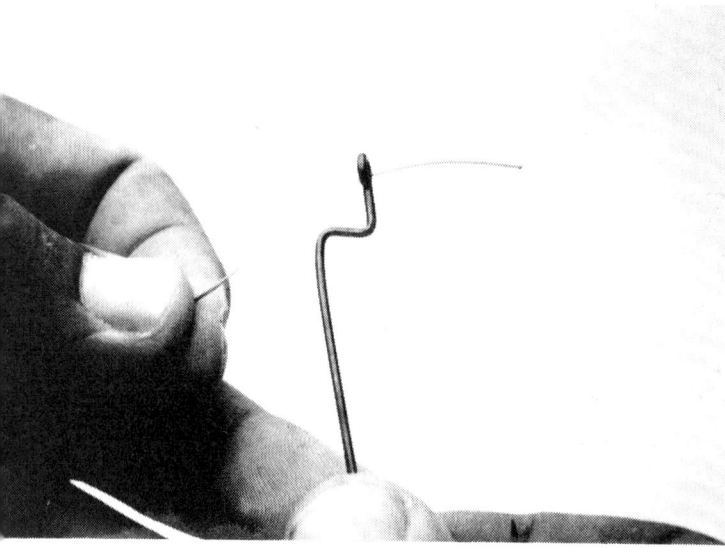

1. Thread monofilament through eye hook from the back side (side opposite hook point). Leave about six inches for wrapping the Burknot.

2. Wrap monofilament snugly on hook shank starting at the base of the hookeye. Take five complete turns in a clockwise direction.

3. Pass end of monofilament back through the hook-eye so the end of the line is on the same side as the running line.

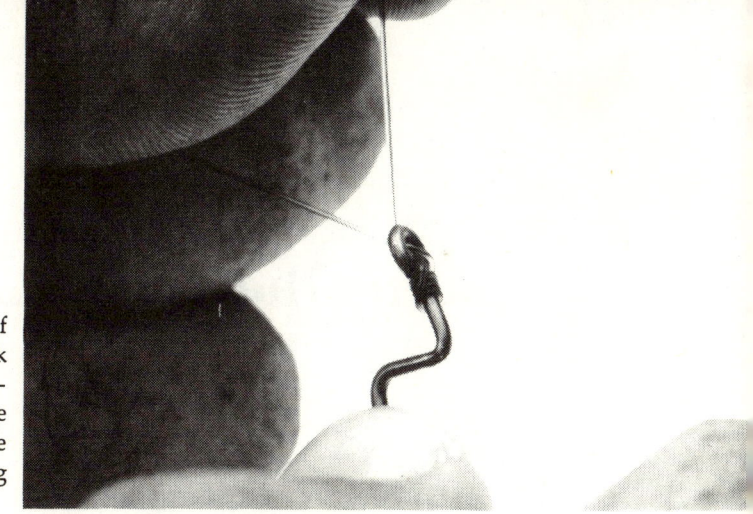

4. Tie two simple loop or cinch knots to secure loose end. Pull the knot into the hook eye.

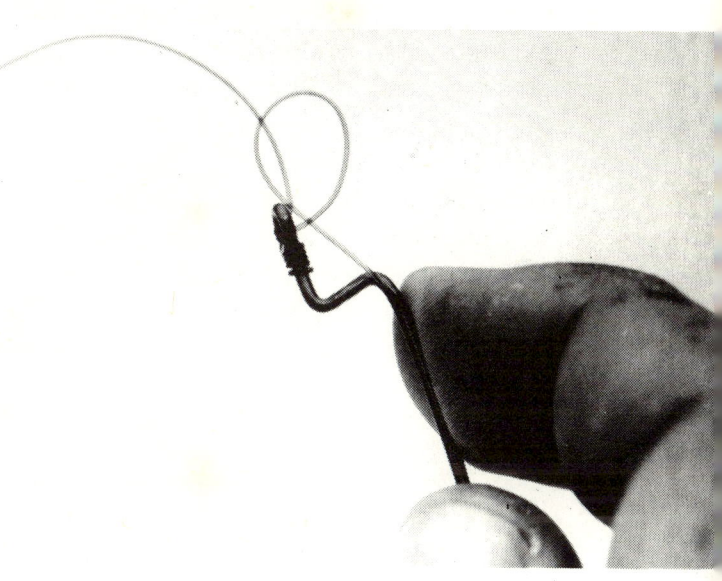

5. Trim loose end, but leave about one-sixteenth inch of line. If slippage should occur, this prevents failure. It also helps hold plastic worm in position.

TIP NO. 60

Curing the Sliding Worm Problem

The most common method of rigging a plastic worm is via the Texas rig. The method is not without fault, but it is the best compromise of good and bad. The most annoying problem is having the worm slide down the hook shank when fishing in brush or when setting the hook. Devices such as barbs on the shank or short pieces of toothpick stuck through the worm and into the hook eye have achieved moderate success but Wayne Cummings, California's bass fisherman *par excellence*, has the best solution to the problem that we've seen.

Take a weedless hook and cut off the weed guard, leaving two short wires about a quarter-inch long. Bend the wires forward over the hook. Rig the worm in the normal manner. Now test it. That worm is on there!

TIP NO. 61

Inside Dope on Fishing

Taking a few moments after the first catch of the day to clean and examine the unfortunate specimen may seem like a waste of precious angling time, but conducting a brief post mortem will greatly increase your chances of catching more fish. An examination of the stomach contents will reveal the foods most recently eaten. You can then use the matching fly or lure, the one most likely to dupe the next fish.

For example, if the fish has been feeding on small minnows, a streamer fly would be your natural choice. Grasshoppers, ants, beetles, or other land creatures are a signal to fish along the bank.

All you have to do is catch that first fish. If the fishing is poor and the first fish is slow in coming, you can always offer to clean somebody else's fish!

TIP NO. 62

A Real Worm Turns

Although the live nightcrawler is considered one of the most common baits, its effectiveness varies with the delicacy of its presentation. For best results, the crawler fisherman must present his wriggling beast as if it were free of all encumbrances.

Light lines are a must. Deep or dark-water fishermen may use lines as heavy as eight-pound test, but the clear-water angler will have to stick with four-pound or even two-pound test mono for best results.

Attached to the end of this line is a #6, #8, or #10 hook which is buried in the very tip of the crawler's nose. If too many strikes are missed or if panfish persistently munch on the other end of the worm, a homemade worm rig is sometimes effective — simply a two-hook rig created by tying about six inches of four-pound mono to the forward hook and adding a #10 tail hook.

The purist crawler man will often fish with no sinkers, preferring to let the worm sink by itself. It's a nuisance to use in deep water, but the worm sinks slowly and naturally; the fish is less likely to drop the bait; and the take is most sensitively transmitted to the fisherman.

But overall it's more practical to use a sinker — either a split shot attached about eighteen inches above the worm, or a slip sinker rig similar to the popular midwest Lindy rig. The Lindy uses a swivel tied into the line about a foot and a half above the bait, which prevents the otherwise free-sliding sinker from reaching the crawler.

Obviously light rigs call for light spinning rods. The pro opts for a light nine-foot spinning rod built on a flyrod blank (like the Fenwick FS110), but a beginner might prefer a shorter stick. You can even use a flyrod if it has a closed-face, under-the-rod reel.

Even with these rods, a standard casting motion will tear the crawler from the hook. Instead, a roundhouse lobbing motion must be used, much like the slow, full-arm beginner's swing.

The nightcrawler is usually kept on a tight line. The reel bail is kept open and the angler maintains tension with his fingertip on the spool. At the first raps, he lifts his finger, allows the fish enough time to take the worm, and then carefully tightens the line and strikes. Hard! If you've got the right rod, you won't break the thin line.

One final note. Much ridicule has been heaped on the air-blown crawler, but as the ads say, it really, *really* works. Put a couple of puffs of air in that crawler's tail with a worm blower, and it will float clear of bottom and be much easier for bass to spot.

TIP NO. 63

Cool Tips for Storing Nightcrawlers

Nightcrawlers are deadly for walleyes, bass, panfish, trout, bullheads — just about any freshwater fish you can name! You'll have most luck with the liveliest and, often , the largest nightcrawlers. Whether you pick your own or buy them from a bait shop, you can store them for months if you observe these rules:

- Store nightcrawlers away from sunlight in cool temperatures, ideally between 45 and 55° F. (Old refrigerators make fine crawler coolers.)
- You can keep crawlers in a variety of containers as long as they have some ventilation. Styrofoam and bead board chests are ideal because they breathe. Some anglers use beer coolers made from these materials; others shallow chests used to transport tropical fish or similar cartons used by bait dealers to carry flats (lots of five hundred) of nightcrawlers. These chests are usually four to eight inches deep and about fifteen inches square, and are easy to stack in refrigerators.
- Prepare a bed for your nightcrawlers by adding water to a commercially manufactured worm bedding. The trick is to moisten the bedding until it's damp, but not dripping wet. Pre-cool bedding before adding crawlers.
- Never use chlorinated water when preparing worm bedding. Obtain clean water from a well, lake or stream, rain or snow, or even from your dehumidifier. If you can find no substitute for chlorinated tap water, allow it to age for a day or longer before using it.
- The moistened bedding should be no more than three or four inches deep. Form a loose mound of bedding in the center of the container, or slope the bedding toward one side, leaving some of the container's bottom exposed. These methods help ventilate the bedding and allow you to spot accumulations of water.
- If you can squeeze more than a few drops of water from a handful of bedding, it's too wet. Add dry bedding to the mixture to absorb excess water.
- Place nightcrawlers on top of the bedding. They can work into the bedding themselves, adjusting to their new environment at their own pace. Look for damaged or weak crawlers.

- Discard dead and questionable nightcrawlers to avoid contaminating the bedding.
- Select natural worm beddings with food. Lindy Little Joe Worm Bedding has always been my favorite. You can periodically renew bedding and crawlers with Lindy Little Joe Worm Food.
- To help keep your worm bedding moist, place damp newspaper on top of it.

Whether you call them nightcrawlers or dew worms, the more care you give them, the more fish they will catch.

TIP NO. 64

Raise Your Own Worms

How would you like a ready supply of bait the year around? Raising earthworms in your basement, backyard, or heated garage is easier than you think. Indeed, it can even be a profitable hobby for a youngster living near fishing waters. Certainly profitable enough to keep him in fishing tackle.

The worms are cultured in a container full of compost. Almost any fairly large container will do, such as barrel halves, old garbage cans, or wooden boxes. A wash tub about two feet in diameter and fifteen inches deep is hard to beat. A worm culture in such a tub can produce two to three thousand worms a year.

To prepare the tub, cut a drain hole about two inches in diameter in the bottom of the tub and cover the hole with wire screening. The compost for the culture should be made of three equal parts of well-rotted manure, peat moss, and good topsoil. The topsoil should not be sandy. Mix these three together well, wetting the peat moss before mixing. Then add a pound of cornmeal to your compost mixture. Next, add a layer of hay or leaves to the bottom of the tub. Fill the tub with the compost mixture to within about four inches of the top. Do not pack the compost down. Leave it loose and porous. Cover the top of the compost bed with two or three layers of burlap, and water the bed with as much water as the compost will readily absorb. The worm bed is now ready.

The most popluar worm for culturing is the red wiggler, a small active species that makes excellent bait for trout, smallmouth bass, panfish, and bullheads. Red wigglers are also excellent bait for ice fishing. Buy about two hundred worms from a bait dealer and place them on the damp bedding. In a short time, they will burrow out of sight.

Feeding is easy. Coffee grounds, cornmeal, cottonseed meal, and even chicken mash are all good. The chicken mash should be placed on top of the compost in bands or rows and never in great quantity or it will sour. The other three suggested worm feeds should be sprinkled over the top of the compost. Feeding once a week is enough. After each feeding, cover the top with burlap and sprinkle with water. Don't over water! The compost bed must not be soggy.

Earthworms are easy to care for. Once they have moist compost and are being fed regularly, all they need is shade in the summer and protection from frost in the winter.

Worm eggs will appear about two weeks after stocking. Three months later your worms will be harvestable. To have them ready for the opening of trout season, culture must be started in January. A few days before harvesting, stop watering. Then, using a spading fork, dig out some of the bedding and pile it on a smooth surface. A plastic garbage bag lying flat on the ground or floor is excellent. Leave the compost pile for a while — the worms will gather toward the bottom for easy picking.

Repeat this until you have harvested most of your worms. For a continuous supply, put the compost back into the tub and start your worm factory again. The harvested worms should be placed in another tub. The compost should be replaced each year, but even then it is useful as a garden soil conditioner.

TIP NO. 65

Tempt Walleyes with Leeches

Leeches are the hot live-bait phenomenon that has everybody agog in walleye country. The best way to fish them is by Lindy Rigging with a plain hook and a slip sinker. Here are some worthwhile tips:
- Make sure you have ribbon leeches, not the soft mud leech or bloodsucker. Bait dealers trap the right kind from non-fish lakes and sloughs, and chances are the leeches you find near your dock will fail to tempt walleyes.
- Choose the large or jumbo leeches, but be prepared to try the smaller ones, especially when fish are finicky. Sometimes it pays to trail several small leeches from a single hook.
- Hook a leech through the sucker end, impaling it only once.
- Troll or drift *slowly*. This allows the leech to swim with a natural, undulating action. Going too fast causes the leech to spin or to pull straight through the water.
- Periodically check the leech to make sure it's trailing properly. Once in a while a writhing leech will tangle with hook and leader.
- Use your Lindy Rig method of feeding line to a biting fish as you would with minnows or nightcrawlers. At the first sign of a bite, release line toward the biting fish. With large leeches, or when fish seem cautious, allow plenty of time before setting the hook; with smaller leeches, or if the fish strikes hard, simply lower your rod tip toward the fish and set the hook.
- Never hesitate to re-use a fresh-looking leech after catching a fish. Leeches are more resilient and tear less easily than nightcrawlers.
- Store leeches in cold water. It is unnecessary to feed them.

TIP NO. 66

Frogs Rarely Fail

There are dog days when even the best-fished artificial lures won't stir any bass to action, regardless of how systematically and diligently they are fished. That's the time for Mr. Frog.

There are probably as many ways to rig a frog to a hook as there are species of frogs. Generally the simpler ones are the best. The simplest is to thread a weedless 50 hook through the frog's lips from the bottom up. When the weed guard is closed, you are in business. At first, fish the frog without any sinkers, allowing it to swim about without restriction.

When casting a frog, toss it out firmly without too much snap of the wrist. It doesn't take much of a snap to tear the frog loose. Side casts are generally better because they don't use as much snap.

There are many frog harnesses on the market, but most have too many hooks. These harnesses are better at catching weeds than bass. Also, frogs hampered by harnesses tend to sit tight. It takes a moving frog to entice a bass to strike.

A couple of the better harnesses available are the threader harness and the loop harness made by Weber. With the threader rig, the frog is hooked through the lips from the top down and through the skin of the abdomen. When the line is tight, the shank of the hook lies parallel to the frog's belly and the hook hangs barb down. A weedless hook can be used for this rig. The Weber harness has a wire loop which is tightened just behind the frog's forelegs, while a weedless hook is threaded through the frog's lips from the bottom up.

During the summer, when the big bass are down in cooler water, I put a sinker about six feet ahead of the lip-hooked frog. The sinker hangs straight down from the bobber and the frog is free to swim six feet from the sinker in all directions.

TIP NO. 67

Keeping Hooked Bait Alive

Lively bait produces more fish. This is a statement that few will argue with. But to keep bait lively, anglers should be more concerned about their hooks than they usually are. Why? Because bait on fine and small hooks generally stay more active and livelier longer. So use the smallest and the finest hooks practical for the task. For example, hooks as light as 2X Fine are strong enough for panfish and pan sized trout.

TIP NO. 68

The Best Bait for Ice Fishing

Through the ice some of the best bait for panfish, particularly bluegills, are worms and grubs; not earthworms but meal worms, corn borers and such. Fortunately, these hot bluegill baits are easy to find.

Roadsides where goldenrod shows through the snow or corn fields where the corn stalks have not been plowed over are good places to look. Goldenrod galls, those ball-like swellings on the stem, are full of small white grubs much loved by bluegills. Simply pick a few of these galls and, when you need bait as you fish, cut them open. Corn stalks in winter are generally infested with corn borer worms. Pick up stalks that have tiny holes in them and split them open. Inside you will find soft worms, another bluegill delicacy.

Old sawdust piles around lumber mills are another good place to look. White grubs, the larval stage of the June bug, can be dug from piles of sawdust. June bug grubs are good for all panfish, even yellow perch. If you live out in the country, you could dump a pile of sawdust somewhere behind an old shed and have a handy source of ice-fishing bait close to home.

Feed mills and grain elevators are also good places to gather live bait in the form of meal worms and yellow grubs. Both are found beneath dampish grain sacks or in dampish grain. A couple of sacks full of moistened chicken or hog feed left in a shed make a fine meal worm and yellow grub hatchery.

Nature has been kind to ice fishermen, at least as far as bait is concerned. As for weather, that's another matter. But when the panfish are biting, who notices the cold?

TIP NO. 69

Deadly Steelhead Bait

Salmon eggs are a natural fish food. They attract by feel or texture, odor, taste, and color. They are gulped down by fry and fingerlings and consumed in vast quantities by mature fish, providing forage for all species inhabiting the same waters. Hordes of trout and char follow salmon runs, as they pour into their natal streams from the ocean and the Great Lakes to feed on loose eggs, swept by the current from the spawning nests. Brown trout, notoriously cannibalistic, raid brook trout beds using teamwork. One brown trout gorges on eggs while its companion plays standoff with the frantic parent. Even bluegills gang up like dead-end kids and hustle lunker largemouth bass off their nests to get at the clutch.

Spawned eggs, jarred from the nest by the current or some other disturbance, generally tumble downstream as singletons. A single egg, impaled on a hook, is the most natural way to fish with salmon eggs.

Matching hook size to the size of the egg, here's how it works:
- Insert the point of a sharpened hook just under the egg skin. Make the hole as small as possible.
- Work the egg up the shank and over the eye.
- Rotate the egg over the hook point.
- Push the egg down on to the hook point.
- Leave visible only the bend of the hook supporting the egg.

If the situation calls for more than one egg, use a small cluster or several singles which can be slipped on to the hook-like beads.

In most situations, a six-pound test monofilament line and a one to three-pound leader are sufficient for trout. Before joining the line and leader, slip a small egg-type sinker, the kind with the hole bored down the middle, on to the line. Then tie the smallest swivel available between the line and the leader. The center hole in the sinker lets it ride up and down the line, but the little swivel prevents it from sliding on to the leader.

This type of rig will allow fish to grab the egg, turn and move off without feeling any undue drag, because the slack line will play through the sinker which, normally, will be lying on the bottom.

Clusters and sacs are gob baits, used primarily for large fish, especially effective in the spring and fall for coho, chinook, steelhead, rainbow and brown trout, sea-run cutthroat, and Dolly Varden.

Cluster eggs, fished loose, are a tacky mass bottled without any artificial covering. They also are the stuffing for egg sacs, made by wrapping a cluster the size of a thumbnail in a three-inch square of maline cloth, a light netting available at dry goods stores. Pulled snug and tight around the cluster, the netting is secured at the top with thread or a piece of bright yarn. Both baits are fished the same way, with sinkers, and allowed to drift freely and close to the bottom.

For clusters use a strong, extra-short shank hook. Tie the leader down the shank of the hook leaving a loop. Impale the cluster on the hook, then work the leader loop around it and pull tight. Many fisherman prefer the same general pattern for sacs, but with a slice in the shank to hold the sac in position.

Because salmon eggs are a natural food, your presentation should follow the free-wheeling pattern of a single egg or cluster traveling the current and close to the bottom. Ideally, the sinker will touch bottom every few feet, while the current lifts and floats the bait. Depending on your ability to read water and detect and avoid snags, you may expend several casts and many long moments observing the action of the current before it carries your bait at the proper speed and into the proper areas.

As in all stream fishing, you must strive for accuracy and cast to cover — brushy and undercut banks, logs, boulders, rocks and every nook and cranny of fishy-looking water in the drift. Work each thoroughly and systematically and in small areas at a time, for these are the holding grounds where fish lie waiting for the current to bring them food.

TIP NO. 70

The Deadly Bait

Lunker bass, northern walleyes, stripers along the Atlantic coast, everglade snooks or the tarpon of the Gulf Coast — all love pork. There is hardly a fish that swims that can resist a serving of pork if it's presented right.

A look into the tackle box of any experienced angler will usually disclose a few bottles of pork rind in several shapes and sizes — pork eels, pork chunks, pork skirts, pork lizards, pork frogs, pork strips — there isn't any substitute for them. Fished alone on a weedless hook or hooked onto wobbling spoons, spinners, jigs, deep running billed lures, or even popping bugs, pork rind increases your chances of taking fish.

Fly fishermen can cast a fly strip on a naked hook as easily as a streamer fly, and give it more darting action on the retrieve. A tiny strip of pork on the hook of a fly rod popper means increased action. Bluegill and crappie will sometimes pluck at the flipping, wriggling tail. When they do, shorten the strip or add a tiny trailer hook.

Many lures are designed for use with pork strips or pork eel, their action bringing out the most tantalizing antics of the rind. Before each cast, glance at your lure to make certain the pork strip is not hung on the hook point, which would spoil its action and nullify any strikes. Stop each cast just before your lure hits the water to keep pork from fouling on the hook. The softer the rind, the more it will dance, dive, and twist as it slithers through the water or crawls along the bottom. Bottom bouncing a jig or heavy spoon with pork eel or pork strip takes bass and walleye as well. Try bouncing the same lures down the ledges and drop-offs.

The black jig and eel combination originated in the South. The pork eel is a long strip of very thin pork rind cut with considerable fat to make it as thick as it is broad, tapering to a point at the tail. Hooked behind a jig and fished slow on the bottom, it's a killer on bass.

TIP NO. 71

Quiet! Fish Can Hear

Water transmits sounds so well that fish have never developed external ears. The sound simply goes through the bones of the skull to the inner ear. Scientists have shown that some minnow species hear up to 7,000 vibrations per second. The catfish can hear up to 13,000 vibrations per second, approaching the 18,000 to 20,000 level for humans. Sharks and rays, incidentally, have poor hearing because their skulls are entirely composed of cartilage which does not transmit sound well.

Fish can hear low-range sounds better than man. Hearing when referring to low-range sounds is perhaps an incorrect term to use because these sounds are felt through the lateral line running from behind the head of the fish along each side to the tail.

What does this mean to anglers? A lot. You can talk or play a radio while fishing. Human voices will seldom reach fish with enough volume to have much effect. But scrape a wire fish stringer along a metal boat, bang an anchor against a gunwale, or walk with heavy feet along a stream bank, and fish will hear it — the sounds now have a medium by which to travel through water. So wear soft-soled shoes when fishing. Don't make any banging and scraping sounds while in a boat. And, above all, approach your favorite trout pools as quietly as if you were stalking a big buck deer.

TIP NO. 72

Careful! Fish Can Smell

A lot of water has passed under the bridge since the day an alert fisheries biologist noticed that every time he immersed his hands in water, the salmon downstream from his fish-tagging nets became alarmed and shied away. This phenomenon led to extensive studies on the smelling capacity of salmon. It was found that some substances, for example salmon blood, whale oil, juniper oil, clove oil, and gasoline had no effect on salmon. They could smell them, but were not afraid of them. But the smell of human hands, dog paws, bear paws, and the flesh of sea lions frightened them. Naturally enough, since all these represent predator odors.

Other studies have shown that fish can detect certain pollutants even in minute quantities and will avoid pollutants if they can. It also led to the formulation of the theory that salmon and other anadromous fish recognize the waters of their home streams by their sense of smell, thus leading them to their home streams to spawn. Each stream, apparently, has a particular odor.

Fish depend on their sense of smell to avoid predators and find food. Every angler knows that the best catfish baits are also the smelliest. Catfish find all their food by a sense of smell and by "taste" through their whiskers and barbels. But, even more important, it was found that fish can detect serine, an acid exuded by humans, in minute parts — down to one part per million.

What does all this have to do with fishing? Just this. Have you ever seen an angler doing everything his buddies are doing, using the same tackle, the same lures or bait, the same technique, but only catching a fraction of the fish? I have. I have fished with such people.

The guy just had bad luck you say? No. Luck had nothing to do with it. The guy is unlucky all right, but it's serine, the hand acid that's to blame. The guy just smells bad to fish. Every time he handles the lure or bait — to tie a new lure on, to clear it of weeds, or to put on fresh bait — he contaminates the lure or bait. He repels fish.

A few years ago, my wife and I and another couple were out to get a mess of skillet-sized bullheads for our breakfast. Everyone in the boat caught catfish but me. I tried the exact same spots as everyone else, but nothing worked. A brain wave hit me. I got my wife to bait my hook with the big night crawlers we were using, and from then on I, too, began catching fish. Since that time, I have tried this with other anglers who were not having any luck when I was catching fish, and their results always improved.

What's the secret? Well, it seems that the biochemical nature of serine not only varies from one person to the next, but also from one day to the next. One day fish may find your hand acid unpleasant; the next day it may have no effect at all. (It is also probable that the serine from some people is unpleasant to fish all of the time.)

The moral of this is not obvious, but it boils down to this: if you are going fishless while your buddies are bringing them in left and right, de-scent yourself and try to cover up the odor of your hand acid. Bring along a bottle of liquid soap and a wash basin to wash your hands as well as your lures — the smell of soap suds has no effect on fish.

Handle your lures as little as possible. Try rubbing your hands with aromatic oils such as clove, vanilla, anise, or sassafras. Try some of the new scented lures. Use rubber gloves to bait your hooks. Try spitting on your lure. Saliva neutralizes hand acid. Just because on some days you are a stinker to fish doesn't mean that you can't catch them. It means you have to try harder.

TIP NO. 73

Fish by the Barometer

Barometer fishing is not new. Many fishermen have tried it and, when they still had fishless days, they promptly forgot about it. There is no such thing as a cure-all for fishless days. Every fisherman has them — even the experts, but the expert has fewer because he has more fishing twists and tricks in his noggin.

The barometer is a fine fishing indicator once you learn how to use it and *if* you realize that fish do not always have the same response to changes in barometric pressure.

Barometric pressure is the relative weight of the atmosphere bearing down on the earth's surface. It is measured on a column of mercury from a standard at sea level. The higher the altitude, the lighter the pressure. The pressure is recorded from thirty inches and it never varies more than an inch below or above. A pressure of 30 to 29 is low, while that of 30 to 31 is high. The inches are divided into tenths by decimals. Thus, a sample low reading would be 29:40.

Each barometer has two needles. The colored needle records the prevailing pressure. You set the other needle on the colored one and look at it periodically. The colored needle will respond to pressure changes and move accordingly. You can tell at a glance if the pressure is falling or rising. This is your clue as to where to fish.

Here is how it works: all aquatic insects hatch at low pressure. Lowering pressure allows the ripe pupa or larva to break out of its fragile skin by internal expansion. The insect pupae nearly always live in shallow water, hence the hatches occur in the shallows. Small baitfish take advantage of this banquet. Game fish follow baitfish and the moral is to fish the shallows when the pressure has dropped to thirty or below.

When the pressure is rising, baitfish go off and hide, while game fish move back into deeper water. They don't necessarily stop feeding, but they switch to feeding on creatures that live in deeper water.

There are two more things that you must know. First, barometric pressure changes with altitude at the rate of one-tenth of an inch for every hundred feet. So if you plan to take your barometer with you to a distant lake, find out its altitude and adjust your barometer accordingly.

Second, regardless of how many insects hatch in times of low pressure, if the water is too warm for a particular species, the barometer won't help you. Barometer fishing works best with the so-called warm-water fish, for example bass.

Here's what you can expect bass to do in the face of changing pressure:
- 30:40 and above — very little action.
- 30:30 — bass will be in old creeks or river beds as deep as forty feet. Try bouncing spoons or jigs with or without trailers. Try live crawfish, salamanders, and large minnows.
- 30:20 — try plastic worms and pork eels at about twelve to twenty feet.

- 30:10 — use diving lures and bottom huggers at about six to twelve feet.
- 29:30 to 30 — work the shallows and edges just below the surface.
- 29:80 to 29:90 — try surface lures and watch for schooling activity offshore.
- 29:70 to 29:80 — fish the windward shores. Try the surface surf. Strong winds are likely at these pressures.
- 29:50 and below — great bass fishing, but storms are probable.

TIP NO. 74

Sonar: A Must for the Sophisticated Fisherman

Sonar is an abbreviation of *SO*und, *NA*vigation, and *R*anging. It was developed as a means of tracking enemy submarines during World War II. Sound is greatly amplified and accelerated when transmitted through water — approximately 4,800 feet per second as compared to 1,100 feet per second through air.

An electrical impulse is converted into a sound wave and transmitted into the water. When the sound wave strikes an obstacle, it rebounds. Since the speed is known and constant, the length of the echo can be measured and the distance to the obstacle determined. One electronic sonar unit can both send and receive the sound waves, as well as time, measure, and record them.

There are several compact portable sonar units on the market for anglers. They are known as fish finders. Many are sensitive enough to reveal the presence of a single fish a hundred feet or more below the surface, if you are skilled enough to interpret what the fish finder is reporting. This takes practice and experience. I, personally, find the sonar to be more useful in finding deep holes, sudden drops, ledges, and other fish-holding spots.

The fish finder transducer sends a high frequency sound wave (inaudible to fish as well as humans) through the water. When the echo returns, the transducer picks it up and converts it back into electrical energy. The unit times the interval and flashes a red signal on the dial. Since the dial is usually calibrated in feet, the signal shows the distance between the transducer and the obstacle that returned the echo.

Fish finders are normally powered by two six-volt lantern batteries contained within an aluminum case. Because they are fully transistorized, the current drain during operation is little more than one-tenth of an ampere.

The transducer transmits sound waves into the water. At the same time, a high intensity neon bulb whirls at constant speed behind the dial on a disc driven by an accurately governed motor. Although capable of firing 10,000 times a second, the discharges are regulated to fire twenty-four times per second at zero on the dial, which gives a constant surface reading. The bulb also fires twenty-four times per second at the point on the dial that indicates the depth, which is determined by the time it takes the sound waves to reach bottom and return. Although the bulb is firing twenty-four times per second, it appears as an almost constant light.

In addition, echoes returned from any object in the water between the surface and the bottom also fire the bulb. Since these echoes are timed, they show the exact depth of any fish, or number of fish in the water. And because the sound waves from the transducer go deep into the water in a twenty-two-degree cone, they tell, within a matter of a few feet, the fish's location, as well as its depth.

Generally, the signal at zero on the dial will show continuously, serving as a reminder that the fish locator is on. One always interprets the depth of the water and depth of the fish by starting with the surface as zero and counting down.

TIP NO. 75

The Downrigger for Deep-Dwelling Fish

Every fisherman knows that many species of fish go deep in the summer, driven there by the warmth of surface water. In the past, the standard way to fish deep was to use big sinkers and heavy lures; or, for lake trout, to use metal or lead-core line. But how can a fish fight when it's carrying a big weight or yards of metal line?

Now there is a way of using reasonably light tackle even for the denizens of the deep. How? With downriggers.

It took the Great Lakes' salmon boom to make downriggers better known on freshwater, but they can be just as useful on small inland lakes. Basically the downrigger is a large reel or wheel, mounted on or near the boat's transom which can hold at least two hundred feet of wire line, marked at ten-foot intervals with white paint. Attached to the end of the line so that it can hang straight down is a weight from five to fifteen pounds. The weight may be solid metal or just a coffee can filled with concrete. Five or six feet above the weight a clip is rigged on to the metal line.

The purpose of the clip is to clasp tightly the main line of the fishing rod. Both the fishing line and weighted wire line are lowered simultaneously to the proper trolling depth. The lure can now be trolled freely about twenty feet behind the boat at an exact depth. When a fish strikes the lure, the trolling line is pulled free of the clip (as with an outrigger) and the fish is free to fight on an almost weightless line. Someone else can reel in the wire line to get it out of the way.

Since no trolling weight or sinker is used, the fight is always between the angler and the fish. Light tackle really makes for fine sport.

TIP NO. 76

Formula for Successful Trolling

For many game fish trolling is the best technique, particularly in big waters. Whether you are fishing on a party boat for coho with six lines overboard or on a small car topper with two lines, the trolling techniques are the same. The trolling tips described here are designed to help the beginner. They refer only to the basics of good trolling know-how. Once mastered, success comes from experimentation and exposure.

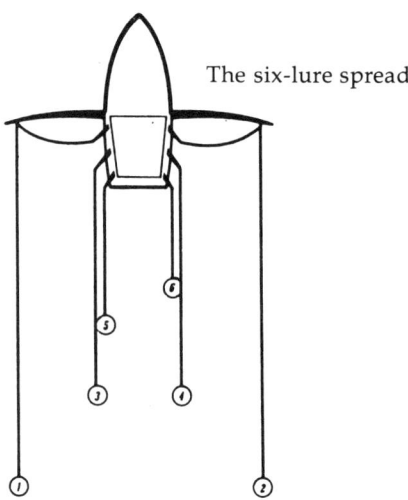

The six-lure spread

The Six-Lure Spread

What follows is based on the use of a six-lure spread such as the ones used on the Lake Michigan coho boats or in saltwater big-game fishing. The first lines to set out are the outrigger lines 1 and 2 (see diagram). Then, set out the mid-ship flat lines 3 and 4. Finally, set out flat lines 5 and 6. Note the layout of the lures. This is a good beginning for the day and, under most conditions, will result in tangle-free trolling.

Be versatile. For example, if lures 3 and 4 are the consistent fish catchers of the day, bring up lures 1 and 2 and drop lures 5 and 6 back to the level of 3 and 4. Thus, when the next fish hook on to lures 3 and 4, there is chance of a fish on all six lines.

Make the mid-ship flat lines 3 and 4 the immediate action rods. For example, a fish that is striking but not connecting with lure 2 might be handled by dropping lure 4 back alongside 2, trying to tease and steal the fish away, then rapidly reeling in, in an attempt to draw the fish into the flat line area where it can be more readily handled — easier said than done, but a lot of fun to try.

Vary the Baits

Game fish are fickle. Until a reliable lure size and color can be established for the day, offer them a choice. When one lure produces more than others, set out at least half the lines with that lure and continue experimenting with the other half.

Keep Hooks Sharp

A sharp hook hitting bone stands a fifty-fifty chance of sliding off into gristle somewhere. A dull hook stands a hundred percent chance of just bouncing off. In salt water even the trolling action alone has a dulling wearing effect on the hook. Before tossing the hook overboard a few swipes with a hook hone are necessary.

The Swivels Must Swivel

A twisted line is the result of a frozen swivel. It is true that an improperly rigged lure that spins is also a major offender and should be corrected, but proper swivel care, with a drop of oil or a replacement from time to time, will keep most twist problems to a minimum.

Vary the Speed

Treat every day differently. If what is usually normal draws a blank, race along with the baits skipping on top, slow down to almost a crawl, troll in a big "S", which will vary the lure speed on the turns. In a slick that seems void of fish, stop and let the lures sink, then speed up, causing the lures to head for the surface. Hopefully, this will bring the fish up after them.

Control Flat Lines

Four free-swinging flat lines can cause problems. The solution is to pin them down. Place the aft rod holders at an increased angle, allowing the two forward lines to ride freely over the

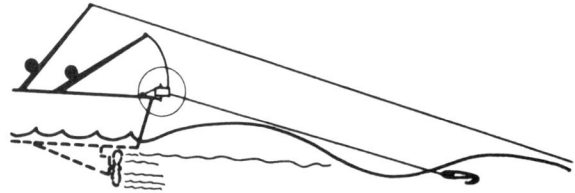

tips of the aft rods. Then, with the use of clothespin-type outrigger pins, pin down the two aft lines to the transom, as illustrated in the diagram. Leave slack between the rod tip and pin to avoid pulling out.

Fight the Fish, Not the Boat

A skipper can use his boat to help the angler set the hook into a big fish, but it is a great disservice to a knowledgeable angler to have to fight any fish while the boat is kept running with any amount of speed. It only results in sore muscles, stress, broken lines, terminal tackle, and bad feelings. Fighting a fish from a dead boat cannot always be advocated but, whenever possible, it's a lot more fun when the fight is just between the angler and the fish.

Keep Everything Compatible

The best trolling success comes only when the tackle, the rod, line, and lure, and the trolling speed are compatible. For example, you may have some slow-speed lures. You may also have fast-speed lures that will troll well at slower speeds. Often, however, although these two lures are compatible at slower speeds, they are not the other way around. Be careful of the lures you use. Put every lure out as though you wanted to catch a world record on it.

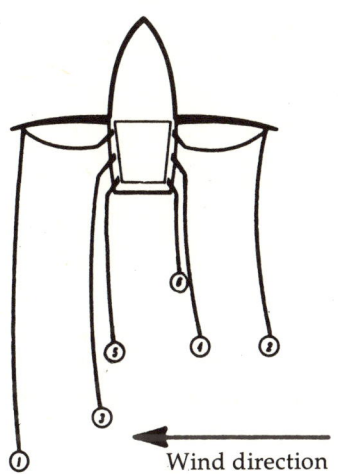
Wind direction

Watch the Wind

Nothing frustrates a skipper more than a group of novice anglers with tangled lines. On those tough, windy days attempt a fairly steady course, placing out the lee side lines first at the longest range. Working windward, shorten each line as illustrated. It's not foolproof, but it usually works. Make your turns to the lee side, being sure to change over on a complete turn.

TIP NO. 77

Try the Countdown for Different Water Levels

The countdown fishing technique is a fine way to fish all water levels systematically. Of course it only works with sinking lures. It is particularly useful in deep water or when you want to keep your lures just above weedbeds or snags on the bottom.

Here is how it works: Make a long cast. When the lure hits the water, reel in all the slack line and start counting at approximately one-second intervals. Keep counting until your lure settles to the bottom. Remember the count. For example, let's say that the lure settled on the bottom at the count of nine. On your next cast, start reeling and working your lure at count eight to keep the lure just off the bottom. Now, systematically fish the water at different levels — using the different counts — slowly working to the surface.

When you get a strike or catch a fish at a certain count, give that water level a good workout. There may be another fish there. This is particularly true for schooling fish species, such as walleye and white bass. This particular water level may be at the optimum temperature. So try it at other places in the lake.

Always hold your rod tip low when working or retrieving the lure. This prevents the lure from coming to the surface as rapidly as it would with a high rod tip. This, the countdown method, works even better with jigging lures fished from a boat or through the ice.

TIP NO. 78

Deep-Running Rigs

Deep-running rigs for walleye and lake trout trolling can be made up for almost any type and depth of water. One fish-taking type consists of a three-way swivel with a sinker on the bottom and the lure on a separate length of monofilament. The lure can be controlled by the length of the line on the sinker. While the sinker bounces along the bottom, the lure travels snag-free just above. Various types of spinners, spoons, and plugs are used in this rig.

TIP NO. 79

How to Ice-Fish with Artificials

I know a man who can't stand live bait — he will not get in the same boat with a minnow bucket, and worms make his skin itch. He's a plug tosser, a jig caster. Artificial lures only. He won't take a fish any other way.

Hates ice fishing, he claims. Can't cast, can't troll, and you can't catch fish with artificials. Sure, casting and trolling may be impossible through ten inches of ice, but don't tell an ice fisherman that he can't catch fish with artificials. It's not so. A winter crappie will take a lure just as quickly as it takes a fathead minnow. Walleyes will grab a lure loaded with treble hooks as easily as a shiner — if you know what you're doing.

And how do you get the right action on an artificial under the ice? Good question. The only way you'll do it is by using lures made for vertical fishing; that is, fishing straight up and down such as through a hole in the ice.

Consider the Jigging lure or Pilkki made by the Rapala people especially for winter angling. These are artificials that will catch fish, and there is no need to dress them up with a minnow.

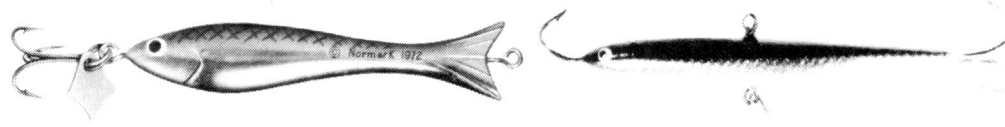

The Finnish jigging lure and the Pilkki are two top lures for ice fishermen. Both prove that you don't need live bait to catch fish through the ice.

The jigging lure is an amazing invention. Minnow-like, it sits horizontally when in the water, perfectly balanced and perfectly painted. Fish will often hit as the lure simply dangles like a groggy minnow. But give the lure action — an up-and-down twitch on the line — and the Jigging lure swims in a tantalizing circular pattern like an injured minnow. It comes in four lengths (1 1/2 to 3 1/2 inches) and three colors (silver, gold, and fluorescent red).

The Pilkki works through the ice on a slightly different principle. The lure hangs vertically in the water. To get the action, raise and drop it quickly. As the Pilkki sinks, it flutters. And, as the lure is raised again, it wobbles like a suffering minnow just hoping to be swallowed. The Pilkki, either in the 1 3/8 inch or 2 1/4 inch size, will take every game fish through ice. The metal lure is available in nickel, copper and brass; in two colors, red and black.

TIP NO. 80

How Not to Do the Twist

Spooling new line to a spinning reel seems to be a simple enough job, but if it's not done properly, the results can be disastrous. With open-face or closed-face spinning reels, the bail or pickup revolves and winds the line to a fixed spool. Because the spool is stationary and the bail revolving, the possibility exists for putting twist in the line if the spooling is not done properly. The method outlined here minimizes twist. Follow it carefully and you'll have a properly filled reel.

Buy the right number of spools to fill your reel.

- When using connected spools, stack them on top of one another so that the line comes off each spool in the same direction. Fasten together with tape, or nails and a rubber band.

- With connected spools, there is one spool which has a loose end of line. If using more than two connected spools, the one with the loose end should always be on the outside. Tie a loop in the loose end, string through the bail or through the opening in the cover on a closed-face reel, and attach to your reel spool.

- This step is key because if the line comes off the spool in the wrong direction, twist will be put in it as it goes on your reel spool. Have someone else hold the spools or put them flat on the ground. Be sure the line comes off in the same direction as the pickup or bail revolves. If the line is unwinding in the wrong direction, turn the spools around. In some cases the line will be coming off the bottom spool first. Actually, since the line spool is stationary, the line really balloons off the end of the spool.

- With your fingers, lightly pinch the line ahead of your reel as you wind. This provides the necessary tension to insure proper spooling. It will also show if any twist is being introduced.
- Wind the line on to the reel. Fill to within roughly one-eighth inch of the edge.

Spooling a new line on to a casting-trolling reel involves the same procedure as that described for a fixed spool reel up to the point of putting the line on the reel. When the spools have been fastened together, insert a pencil through the center to serve as an arbor so the spools can rotate easily. Have someone hold the pencil or hold it in a vise. Fasten the free end of the line on the reel spool and wind it on to the reel from the side of the hundred-yard spools as they revolve about the pencil. Pinch the line ahead of the reel to ensure proper tension.

TIP NO. 81

Getting Out the Twist

If the line on your reel gets twisted, let it drag out behind a boat without a lure. This action will straighten out most twists.

TIP NO. 82

Using Marked Line

I have found line marked at five-foot intervals to be useful so often and for so many different kinds of fish that I habitually keep two spools from my favorite spinning reel loaded with marked line. By counting the marks, I can regulate the depth of my lure. If six marks have gone out, meaning we are trolling thirty feet of line, I can continue to fish at this depth as long as we maintain a constant speed.

A word of warning: with monofilament line and any given lure or a sinker of any given weight, you can only fish so deep. Contrary to the old bromide, beyond a certain point your lure won't work deeper and deeper as you let out more line. Instead, the line forms a parabolic curve within and under the water; trolling fifty yards of line may not get your lure one inch deeper than trolling fifty feet. Skin friction of water on the line will put more resistance on the line and tend to straighten it, causing the bait to run more shallowly. This is especially true with non-metallic lines, such as monofilament.

TIP NO. 83

Be a Tippet Switcher

Wrong leaders have discouraged more would-be flyfishermen than any other problem. If a leader is not stiff and heavy enough in the butt, and is not then correctly tapered down to a proper fine tippet, it will *not* carry forward the flyline's thrust and will *not* turn over smoothly and lie out straight. At worst, it will fall down in a nasty tangled wad. At best, it will let your fly go sailing crazily around, to alight nowhere near the spot you intended.

So a leader (which costs only pennies) is vitally important. The front twenty percent of it, the tippet, is the business end of the whole rig (your arm, your rod, the flyline, the leader... butt, balanced taper and *tippet* to which is attached the fly). The tippet is critical: it must be exactly right or the whole chain of operation collapses.

Since the tippet must be right, it follows that no single tippet can be perfect for all fishing.

Let's begin with the obvious. A fine 5X tippet with a big fat Size 6 wind-resistant streamer tied to it is not going to begin to have the guts to transmit your flyline's energy and lay that fly out straight. It's going to collapse in a wad.

Conversely, a husky fat 1X tippet could never be fitted through the eye of a Size 20 fly and, if it could, the fly would be dragged around on the water like a helpless little bug affixed to the end of a stiff broom straw.

Below is an approximate table of correct tippet sizes for corresponding correct fly sizes:

Use tippet size	for fly size
0X(.011")	2 to 1/0
1X(.010")	4,6,8
2X(.0097")	6,8,10
3X(.0087")	10,12,14
4X(.007")	12,14,16
5X(.006")	14,16,18
6X(.005")	16,18,20,22
7X(.004")	18,20,22,28

Obviously, if you have been fishing happily upstream with a No. 16 Adams dry on a 5X leader and arrive at a fast rapids in which you wish to fish a No. 12 Gray Ghost streamer, you know your 5X leader should be a 3X. The 5X is weak for a good fish in fast water and unnecessary for a deceptive free float or invisibility in that water. Furthermore, laying out a big streamer on a fine tippet wrecks the easy casting rhythm which is flyfishing's major pleasure. It means straining and pushing to make the big fly lie out straight.

Okay, so you already knew all about everything said so far. But now the crucial question. Are you in fact, an instant and unhesitating tippet-switcher? Do you really and truly tie a new tippet on to the front of your leader as easily and quickly as you change a fly; *and* with the awareness that your tippet change may well be as important as changing a fly? Think about it.

You should always carry tiny, flat twenty-five-yard spools of tippet material ... the essentials for trouting being one each of 0X, 1X, 3X, 5X, and 7X. An eighteen-inch front tippet does for seven and a half-foot leaders, twenty-inch for nine-foot leaders, twenty-eight-inch for twelve-footers. So each little twenty-five-yard spool lasts you a long time.

The only real tippet-switcher is the guy who can tie a barrel knot quickly and easily. There is no knot-tier in the world more clumsy or butter-fingered than I. So if I can do a barrel knot easily, anybody can. And I can do it like pie. It's a matter of practice, which is steadily maintained because I switch tippets one or two or three times during almost any fishing expedition. I change tippets automatically with a change in fly size or particular water or shift from dry fly to going under with a nymph.

You know the barrel knot. It looks like this:

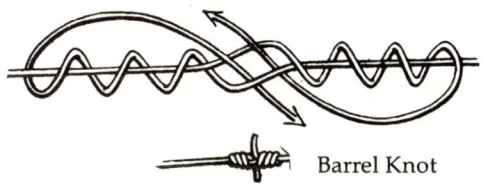

Barrel Knot

I can tie it now while standing knee-deep in rushing water.

I switch tippets not to be fancy, but because a correct tippet makes casting easy and rhythmical instead of pushy and strained. Also because a long fine tippet with a tiny fly in still, clear water, then a shorter, fatter tippet to keep a bottom nymph down catches more trout.

It's easy. It costs next to nothing to carry along a set of the little flat tippet material spools. It makes fishing pleasanter and more productive. If you haven't been enough of a tippet-switcher, try it this season.

TIP NO. 84

How to Fly Fish with a Spinning Rod

A plastic bubble will make a spinning rod perform most of the tricks of a flyrod, including dry fly, streamer, nymph, and similar light lures. Before using the bubble, you must fill it through a tiny hole with either water or mineral oil. To do this, use an eye dropper. Most anglers prefer to use mineral oil because it doesn't evaporate. It's a good idea to make up a set of bubbles of various weights at home so that you have them ready for the various casting conditions you will meet. For example, if you are out casting into the wind, you will need a fairly heavy bubble. If the wind is behind you, a light bubble may be better. There are also times when you will want a bubble that is more than half full so that it will sink. In some instances, you may even need to add one to three BB shots when you are working a swift stream. Since the stopper used to close the hole in some bubbles has a habit of working itself free and popping out while casting, seal it with one or two coats of fingernail polish.

For dry fly angling and near-surface wet fly and nymph fishing, attach the bubble to the end of your regular spinning line. Now add a length of about three or four feet of lighter line to the bubble. Attach a simple dropper leader at about the middle for one fly, and add a second fly to the end of the line. You can tie one, two, three or more on short leaders spaced at appropriate distances ahead of the bubble. With the normal case of casting, the combination won't tangle on the cast or during the float. The use of more than one fly will help determine the fly patterns that the fish are taking. Quite often, experienced spin-fishermen use a dry fly on the dropper leader and a wet or hatching nymph pattern on the end, particularly during the spring hatching season.

When you cast with this rig, use a side cast rather than a conventional overhead cast since you have to have the flies and the bubble out beyond the tip of your rod. Don't snap the cast, but swing it out gently over the water in one continuous motion. If the sweep isn't slow, the rig will twist and tangle. If greater distance is required or if you are fighting a breeze, fill the ball with enough water or mineral oil to weigh it down sufficiently, but not enough to sink it out of sight.

TIP NO. 85

Bunker Dunking for Big Stripers

Live-lining, or fishing for striped bass with live bait, is not new. That's the way the game began two or three hundred years ago. But like most things, it fell out of fashion. Recently though, there has been a flurry of live-bait fishing for striped bass along a good part of the north Atlantic coast from Hatteras to Cape Cod.

The concentration of this rebirth has been in the region of the New York Bight, particularly off the eastern end of Long Island. Here, the preferred bait is the live bunker, mossbunker, or menhaden, three of the more than sixty names by which this oily foodfish is known. Other baitfishes often work just as well. The blackfish or tautog is a good bass bait and up the coast from Long Island, the other Yankees seem to prefer live mackerel to bunker.

Striped bass are especially fond of bunker and spend most of their lives, especially while migrating, following and feeding on the massive schools of menhaden as they move up and down the coast. That's the main reason why bunker are used so readily as a bait. The second reason is that large striped bass prefer big baits and the bunker fills the niche. Thirty to sixty-pound stripers on bunker are not rare catches.

Getting bunker can be a chore. If you have commercial pound traps in your area, be there when the fishermen lift their nets. If not, arm yourself with a light spinning rod and a gang of treble hooks and chase the birds as they follow schools of bunker. Once caught, you must keep them alive. Bass will take dead bunker, but they prefer them live nine times out of ten. A large bait-well, well aerated or with a constant flow of seawater is needed to keep the fish alive.

Along the northern coast of New Jersey and along most of the south shore of Long Island, bunker are fished live, dead, or recently dead. The technique is to slip a 50 O'Shaughnessy hook through the eyes of a dead bunker, ease your boat almost on to the beach, drop the bunker over the side, and back the boat off with the reel in free spool. Travel as long as you have line left on your spool. Then, engage the clutch and slowly drag the dead bunker across the bottom until it is against the boat. Repeat until a bass appears.

Along the Jersey coast, dead bunker is also trolled very slowly so that it just eases across the bottom, clearing the rocks. But along the eastern end of Long Island, off Montauk and Orient Points, and along the eastern Connecticut and Rhode Island coasts, bunker is fished alive. Here, the skipper picks a spot where the tide runs over a shoal off a point of land with a bit of deep water on one side. The boat stems the tide so that the speed of the craft just equals that of the moving current and the live bunker is slipped back and forth over the boulders and through the eddies that build in such an area.

Stemming the tide is usually done with less than a hundred feet of line off the transom. I prefer a dacron or monofilament line of a twenty or thirty-pound-class rod. The line test seldom need be heavier than thirty-pound, even for the biggest bass. To be fished properly, the terminal rig for live bunker dunking takes some effort. I prefer a 6/0 treble hook attached to about two feet of wire leader. The hook is added to a ring and the ring to a barrel swivel before being attached to the metal leader.

Bluefish are equally fond of bunker, hence the metal leader. They also have a nasty habit of chopping off the tail of the bunker. To discourage their coming back again and again, add a drop leader off the ring, on a short eight to ten-inch piece of wire with a second treble hook. Leave it to dangle free. Pass the first treble through the nostrils of the bunker. In this way, the bunker can still breathe and will stay alive for quite a while. The single treble in the head is all that is needed to catch stripers because they usually take a bait headfirst.

This rig is fished rather short — fifty to seventy-five feet of line in about twenty-five or thirty feet of water. The bunker need be only under the surface because bass will rise to such a tempting offer. To keep the bunker down, use from one to four ounces of lead on a beaded drail, added ahead of the wire leader so it will not give a hooked bass something to throw about. The various weight drails are changed as the tide increases or decreases.

The rig is fished in free spool, with the click on and the rod in a holder if you are fishing alone. In free spool, the click may not be enough to hold the bunker and you may have to engage the clutch and set the drag very lightly. A bass will hook itself most of the time; you can adjust the drag after you set the hook.

TIP NO. 86

A Trick for Minnow-Chasing White Bass

When white bass are chasing schools of small minnows on the surface, they frequently refuse spoons, spinners, or jigs fished in the conventional way. That's the time to rig up a medium-sized popping topwater plug with about sixteen inches of monofilament line behind it. Then tie two small panfish-sized jigs — one at the end of the monofilament and the other about halfway to the plug. It's a good idea to have each jig a different color; white and yellow are my favorites.

Cast out where you think the white bass are feeding and play the plug vigorously across the surface. The white bass will be attracted to the popping of the plug, but they will nail the jigs darting just below the surface where they snap at minnows. Doubles are not unusual with this rig when among white bass in a feeding frenzy.

TIP NO. 87

When the Bass Aren't Biting

What do you do when everything on your favorite bass water seems right, but isn't? You know those days — the water is clear, a gentle wind creases it just enough to obscure your shadow, and your casting has never been better — but you just aren't getting any action.

The bass have either stopped feeding or have retreated to remote haunts. What to do? I go to a lighter line and smaller lures. Instead of the usual twelve-pound line I prefer, in log and stump-infested bass water, to drop to eight pounds. I switch to lures in the $1/4$ to $1/8$-ounce weight range, including jigs, spinners, and minnow-shaped plugs. I use the lures systematically, trying different color combinations. When I catch my first bass, even a little one, I look at its contents to see what it has been eating — it could be a tip as to what lure to use.

Plastic worms are my next weapons and I fish them around all over, paying particular attention to deeper holes or any point where the water deepens suddenly. I begin with big black worms nine inches long and slowly work down to three-inch worms on smaller hooks. Again I am quite systematic in presenting the plastic worms in all colors to give the bass a choice.

I also try to fish all the little bays and retreats, regardless of how log-infested and water-lily-covered they are. But here I switch to water-slurping topwater lures and frog imitations. I keep very quiet so as not to unduly alarm the fish. I vary my retrieving speeds from slow, with a few twitches, to ultra-fast. The fast retrieves sometimes make a bass mad, even when he is not in a feeding mood.

If, despite all these efforts, you strike out, don't lose any sleep over it. We all have it that way sometime; just be thankful that you were able to spend the day fishing.

TIP NO. 88

Spinnerbait Basics for More Bass

Spinnerbaits have been around for a long time, but only recently have these attractive lures spun their way to glory. Spinnerbaits combine the leadhead jig concept with one or more spinners to give the bass angler genuine versatility. With spinnerbaits one can employ a variety of retrieves to take bass in all seasons and at all depths.

Here are some tips:

When choosing spinnerbaits, an important consideration is size — especially the size of the blades and the weight of the lure. Blade size helps determine the bait's rate of drop, its sound, and its appearance. Weight also affects the rate of drop, along with casting distance and the ability to fish different depths.

Large blades are most effective when bass hit on a slow drop, when they're going for fast-moving spinnerbaits, and when sound is more important than sight, as in murky water or at night.

Smaller blades are often your best choice when bass prefer fast-dropping lures, when fishing deep water, and when casting into heavy wind.

- Tandem spins (two blades in line) are meant to be buzzed just under the surface in shallow water. When bass are hitting fast-moving spinnerbaits, use the bigger blades with a steady retrieve. Engage your reel and begin your fast retrieve as soon as your lure hits the water.
- When fishing intermediate depths, say five to ten feet, vary your retrieve. Try cranking the spinnerbait fast and then suddenly let it drop toward the bottom as if injured.
- Spinnerbaits can be fished in deep water. Many anglers favor single spins in water over six feet deep. Depending on depth and the desired speed of drop or retrieve, you can use baits as heavy as half an ounce or more.
- In cold water conditions bass often prefer falling spinnerbaits. When a bass grabs a spinnerbait on the drop, it'll feel like a bass inhaling a plastic worm — a slight tap. So be attentive and set the hook at the first sign of that tap!
- When fishing the shallows in very clear or calm water, avoid spooking bass. Use lighter spinnerbaits — $1/4$ and 3/16-ounce sizes.
- It pays to buy well-built spinnerbaits. Cheap tin blades won't give you the results you get from quality blades. Certain rubber skirts gob up and even melt together; better plastic skirts stay straight and untangled.
- Sometimes you'll catch more bass by dressing your spinnerbaits with live bait or artificial offerings. Try pork strips, plastic worm tails, grub tails, or the enticing Lindy Swirl Tails. Skirtless spinnerbaits are effective when teamed up with two to four-inch shiner minnows.

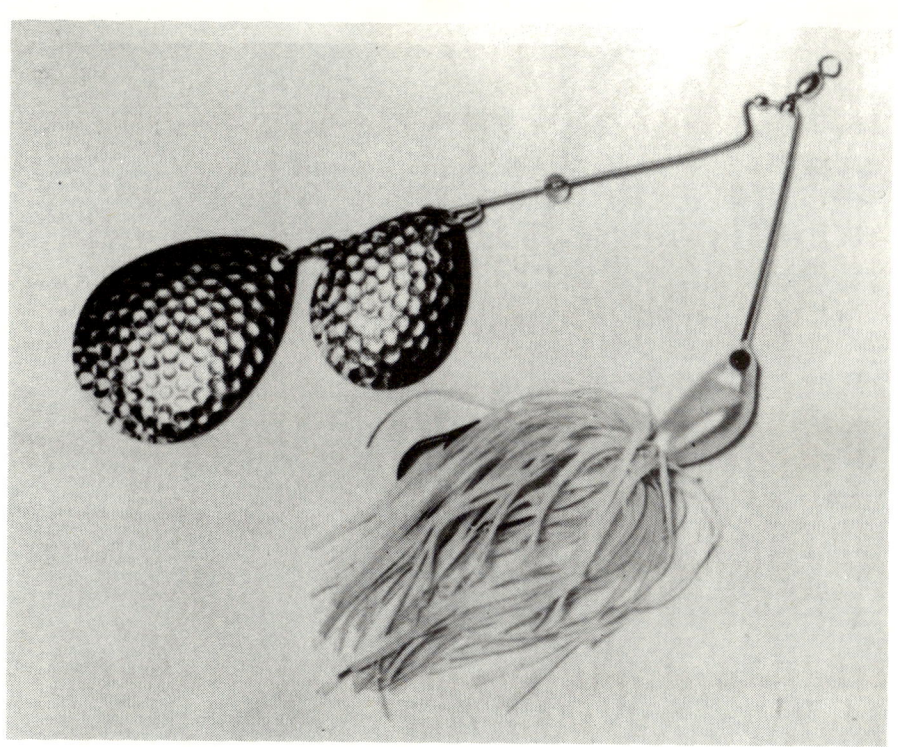

Spinnerbaits have become favorites. When fishing with spinnerbaits in intermediate water depths — 5 to 10 feet — crank the spinnerbait fast for a few feet and then let it drop to the bottom.

TIP NO. 89

Tandem Hooks for Small Spinnerbaits

It's a well-known fact that the first and second Bassmaster Classics were won by Robert Murray and Donald Butler, respectively. Both were using spinnerbaits. Don Butler used a small spinnerbait called the Small OkieBug — SOB for short.

When Butler is getting short strikes or wants to use a small trailer, such as a piece of pork rind or plastic worm tails, he slips a long-shanked hook over the hook of his spinnerbait. To the second hook he attaches a small clump of dried or white bucktail. He also slides a plastic ring over the lure hook to hold the trailer. The plastic ring can be made by cutting a piece of tubing, or it can be obtained from OkieBug, 3501 South Sheridan Road, Tulsa, Oklahoma 74145.

The result is an extremely slick and sometimes very effective trick that every bass man should have in his repertoire. At times it's an ideal way of improving the effectiveness of small spinnerbaits.

TIP NO. 90

Fish the Windward Shore

One of the things I learned early on and almost entirely by accident is that on windy days the windward shore is usually the most productive. It took several years, including a year of university biology, to find out why.

The wind and waves cause plankton to drift toward the windward shore. Small baitfish, minnows, and the like follow the plankton because it is their main food source. Game fish in turn follow baitfish. I have found this to be true for many fish species — panfish such as white bass, white perch, and yellow perch, smallmouth bass, walleye, brook trout, and lake trout when they are still in shallow water in the spring, and even ouananiche, the leaping landlocked salmon.

Some anglers don't believe this, but I have actually seen this phenomenon on a fish finder. First the instrument shows plankton followed by small fish, and then small fish followed by big fish.

Don't expect the fish to be on the windward shore as soon as a strong wind comes along. Give it time. Plankton drift slowly and fish have to alert themselves to the situation. It takes at least a day of sound blowing, but two or three days are better.

Remember, fish frequently face into the waves, but even more often swim parallel to the shore while looking for lunch. So cast or troll into the wind or across the wind. Casting will mean using heavy lures with fair sectional density. Forget the lures that offer big surfaces for the wind to catch.

I have found that the more productive lures at this time are those the same color as the baitfish. It makes sense, doesn't it? After all, if the baitfish are feeding, they are feeding on minnows. Give the 'wounded minnow' lures a try.

When a big blow comes out to a lake, don't pick the comfortable lee shore where casting is easy and where your hide is sheltered. Put on a snug windbreaker and face the wind. You'll catch more fish.

TIP NO. 91

Never Say Die

Often on a fishing trip fishermen are cursed with bad weather. The water is too high or the temperature is too hot. Nearly always, however, they have never really given fishing a proper try. They usually just lament about their bad luck, stay in camp, and drink beer. It takes a dedicated and experienced angler to take advantage of unusual conditions.

A heavy rain following a prolonged dry spell nearly always increases feeding activity among fish, particularly in streams. As water rises a little, fish tend to lose their shyness and feed voraciously. During long periods of high water, however, fishing tends to be slow and hard. That's the time to try smaller feeder streams with less run-off. Beaver ponds and sheltered areas in the headwater of your stream are also worth a try. Fish may be staying here to get relief from murky water.

A prolonged spell of hot weather may heat up the surface water and drive the fish into the deeper water of lakes or to the cool, spring-fed feeder streams. The base of white-water rapids is another good bet. White-water always has plenty of oxygen and fish require more oxygen when the water is warm.

Be innovative. The old cliché about necessity being the mother of invention is true. Certainly sitting around the camp feeling sorry for yourself won't get you any fish.

TIP NO. 92

The Next Fish You Catch May Be a Record Fish

The wise angler, no matter where or how casually he is fishing, should always keep in mind the possibility of catching a record-class fish. This means that at all times lures, lines, rods, and reels should be ready for such a fish. Also, every fisherman should know what to do if he does manage to boat a fish of such heroic size.

Many sad tales abound about the angler who caught a really big fish but, not realizing what he had, failed to have it weighed and verified before eating it.

What should you do? Here are the steps:
- If there is reason to believe the fish is of record class, try to keep it alive or, if this is not possible, get it on ice as soon as possible. If this means pulling anchor and heading back to the dock in the shank of the day, that's okay. One doesn't catch such a fish very often.

- Get the fish weighed as soon as possible, because when fish die, they lose weight through dehydration. Not just any scale will do. Portable scales and scales at most boat docks are not accurate. Meat market scales, checked periodically for accuracy, are best.
- Get witnesses for the weighing. Disinterested parties, as reliable as possible, should be asked to look on. Good witnesses are clergymen, judges, policemen and so on; the very best are game wardens or Fish and Game Department personnel.
- Get the fish verified as to species and have it measured (length and girth) by a qualified person, such as a game warden or Fish and Game Department employee.
- Photograph the fish with the fish lying on grass or on a dock with a yardstick or an extended tape measure beside it.
- Find out all the honors for which the fish may be in line. In addition to the national records kept by *Field and Stream Magazine*, many states and provinces have their own record lists. These are most commonly kept by the Fish and Game Department. Some states and provinces also maintain a master angler list in which they honor persons catching unusually large fish.

Many resorts, lake associations, and promotion-minded corporations recognize catches of large fish and some award handsome prizes for the largest in various categories. Marinas, tackle stores, and fishing lodges stock entry forms and rules for these awards. Many of the major lure manufacturers also honor persons who catch large fish with their lures. Send the company details on where and when the fish was caught, which lure was used, and the weight, length, and girth of the fish. Include a photograph.

In addition to its world record list, *Field and Stream Magazine* each year conducts a fishing contest and honors fishermen taking the season's largest fish. Gold, silver, and bronze pins are awarded to division winners and badges and certificates are given to all persons making certain minimums. For applications forms and rules for the contest, write: Fishing Contest Editor, Field and Stream Magazine, 383 Madison Avenue, New York, New York 10017.

TIP NO. 93

Give the Taxidermist a Break

For most of us, catching a trophy fish is a once in a lifetime experience. The best way to remember it is to have the fish mounted by a good taxidermist. There are many highly qualified people throughout North America, and once you have found a good one, it's worth the extra effort required to send fish long distances if necessary rather than taking a chance on someone who might ruin your trophy. When selecting a taxidermist, find one who has had experience with the type of fish you want to mount. If possible, see his work first.

After you catch your trophy fish, take the following steps: Handle it carefully. Don't let it hang for a long period of time. Don't let it get bashed around. As soon as possible, take several close-up photographs to show its color and shape. If a freezer is available, use it, but first wrap the fish in cloth and a plastic bag. Under no circumstances should the fish be cut in any way before freezing. When you get the chance, contact your taxidermist for further instructions.

If a freezer is not handy and you're not near a good taxidermist, the procedure is different. First, take the photos of the fish, and, as soon as you can, trace its outline on a piece of paper. Next, decide how you would like to have your fish hung. In other words, decide which side of your fish you'd like against the wall. Turning the fish on its good side, make an incision right down the middle of the side you want against the wall and carefully skin your fish. After you have cut down the side of your trophy, most of the skinning is done by pressing your fingers between the flesh and the skin. Pieces of flesh left on the skin are easily removed by scraping with a large spoon.

Cut the carcass free behind the head and in front of the tail, leaving the fins intact and the head and tail attached to the skin. Remove the gills and eyeballs from the head, carefully salting the entire skin with lots of salt. Next, roll the skin up and place it in a plastic bag. Keep it as cold as possible and as soon as you have the opportunity, freeze it. The next step is to send it to your taxidermist, supplying him with the colored photographs and traced outline of the fish. If you follow these instructions, your chances of getting a mount to be proud of are excellent.

TIP NO. 94

Dry Hands Are Best

It's time to dispel the old belief about handling fish. The old timers said wet your hands before reaching for a fish, particularly trout, so that the chances of harming it would be decreased. Wrong! Wet hands make fish even more slippery, forcing you to take a tighter grip. Several years ago studies were conducted to test the damage done to fish by handling them with wet and dry hands. The percentage of fish surviving was greater with dry hands. Why? Don't dry hands remove mucus from the fish scales, exposing the fish to disease and fungus? Yes, but the mucus is quickly replaced by the fish because it secretes this substance almost continuously.

Biologists discovered that the tight grip from wet hands frequently caused internal injuries from which the fish died. So keep your hands dry to insure that the fish you release has a greater chance of living.

TIP NO. 95

Artificial Respiration for Fish

Its sounds strange when someone talks about giving a fish artificial respiration before releasing it after a long battle; however, this is what you must sometimes do if the fish is to survive. Fish must have oxygen. The oxygen content in fast-moving water or just below a set of rapids is much greater than in still water; one reason why fish will take up a lie in these areas.

Under the protective gill covers, the gills are made up of rakers that strain the water of any hard particles before it flows past the gill filaments that actually do the breathing. It is the filaments that release waste carbon dioxide from the system and filter fresh oxygen from the water. Oxygen is assimilated through a thin layer of skin and enters the capillaries where it is carried by the blood stream.

Some fish, for example the tarpon, have a primitive lung that enables them to gulp air out of the atmosphere, holding it in their mouths until it passes through the moist gill filaments. This is why you see tarpon rolling on the surface or gulping air while you're trying to land them.

When a fish is exhausted after tangling with an angler, it has used up its supply of available oxygen. It is the same feeling that you would experience if you ran uphill for a couple of miles. Since more and more sportsmen are releasing game fish to fight another day and perhaps provide sport for someone else, these fish should be turned loose correctly. Always place the fish in the water gently. If it isn't too tired, it will swim right out of your hands. Otherwise, move the fish back and forth slowly through the water, forcing oxygen and water through the gills. When the fish has recovered sufficiently, you will feel it.

With big fish, simply hold your quarry alongside the boat and move the boat slowly ahead. You'll create the same effect of forcing water through the gills and the fish should survive. Remember that the gills of a fish are delicate and the fish can be inadvertently injured if you put your hands under the gill covers while unhooking it. With smaller fish, you can usually get a secure grip by reaching your hand over the back of the head and holding the gill covers closed.

You will also discover that a towel or an old rag helps in gripping a fish without hurting it. On delicate species like trout, you can usually leave the fish in the water, hold the hook or fly between thumb and forefinger, and shake the hook until it comes out.

TIP NO. 96

How to Remove an Imbedded Hook

I don't think there is a real honest-to-goodness fisherman who has not had to remove an imbedded hook from a fishing companion, a stranger, or even from some part of his own anatomy. If you are ever called upon to perform this delicate task, don't reach for a knife, scalpel, or razor blade. Cutting is painful and dangerous. Use the snatch-out method, for which the only tool you need is a loop of fishing line.

Follow these simple steps and the victim will be able to resume fishing immediately, with little discomfort and no worry of infection.

- Remove the hook from the lure if at all possible.
- Make a foot-long loop of line testing about thirty pounds. If your line tests thirty pounds, then a single loop will do. If your line tests fifteen pounds, then double it to make the loop. Ten-pound test line should be triple-stranded.
- Place the loop around the back of your hand and bring it out between your thumb and forefinger. Place the loop over the shank of the hook and gently snug it against the bend of the hook.
- Exert pressure on the hook eye, pushing downward and outward toward buried barb. The moment this pressure is applied, snatch out the hook with a vigorous jerk of the loop. Only a tiny hole remains.
- To prevent infection, apply an antibiotic salve in sufficient amount to cover the wound. Apply a plastic strip bandage, and it is done.

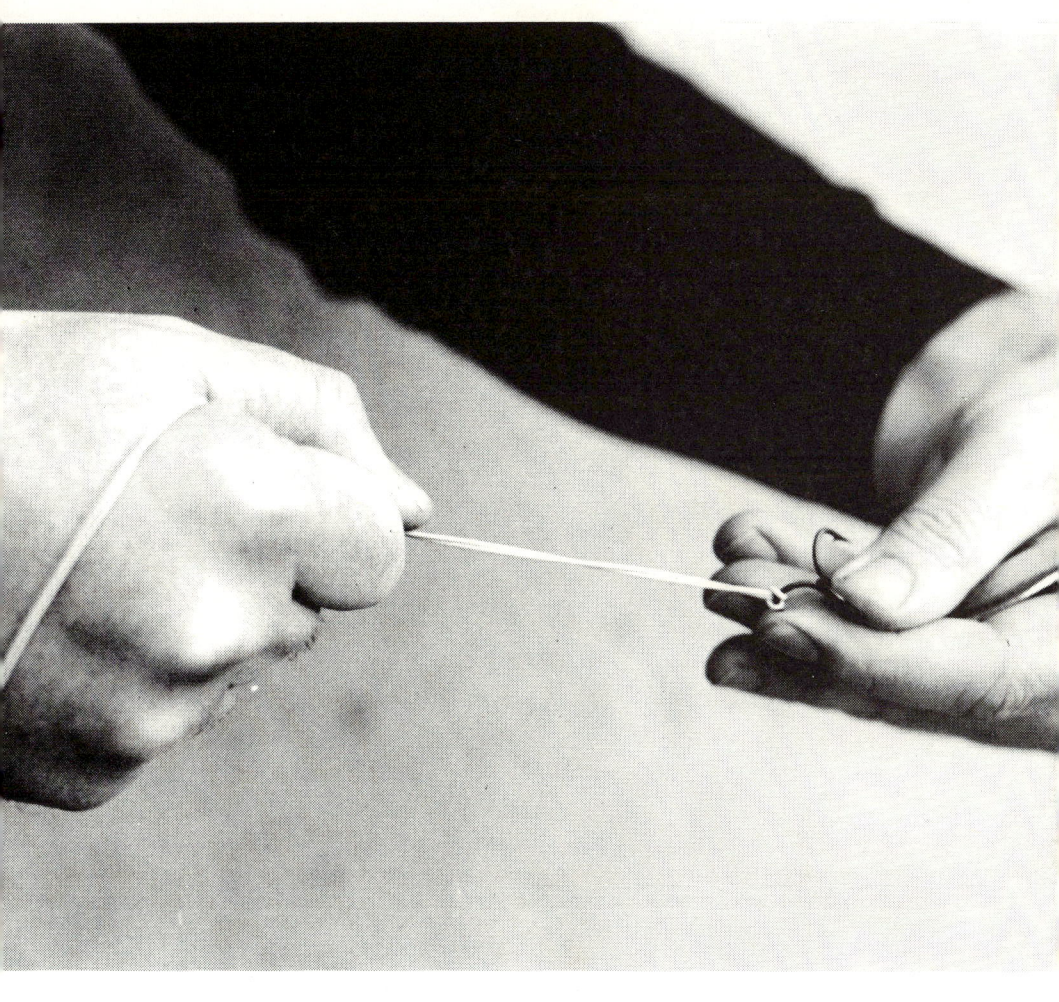

Exert pressure on the hook eye, pushing downward and outward.

The amazing thing about this treatment is the lack of after-pain, due, of course, to germ prevention. The following day the victim is hardly aware he has a wound.

One word of caution. If a hook is buried around an eye or in a large blood vessel, don't attempt any treatment except to apply a clean compress to stem bleeding. Get to a doctor fast.

TIP NO. 97

Cleaning Panfish

Panfish, with the exception of jumbo yellow perch, are generally too small to fillet. They are normally cooked whole, minus the head and tail. The dedicated fisherman should be well equipped to clean fish — a big board, a sharp knife, and a scaling tool. Light cotton gloves are also handy. Fish are easier to grasp with a gloved hand and the gloves prevent scratches from spiny dorsal fins.

Here is the fastest, neatest way to clean panfish:

- Briskly scale the fish with the scaling tool. Do this under running water to keep the scales from flying all over. But be sure to put a screen in the sink drainhole to avoid plugging up the drain with fish scales. With most fish, scaling from tail to head goes faster.
- Cut out the vent (anus) with a "V" cut.
- Hold the fish belly down on the board and cut through the spine just behind the head. Don't cut through the entrails of the fish.
- After severing the spine, push and twist on the head with one hand and pull on the body. The head will come loose with all of the entrails attached.
- Cut off the fins and wash fish well. It's now ready for the pan.

TIP NO. 98

How to Skin a Fish

Some fish taste much better unskinned, while others, like the catfish, have to be skinned.

Here is how: Make a circular cut not much more than skin deep completely around the fish, just behind the gills. Then make two more skin deep cuts, one along the back to the tail and the other down the belly to the tail. Take a corner of the skin on the back of the fish with a pair of pliers and pull the skin tailwards with one smooth motion. Repeat on the other side. With a bit of practice, it takes only a few seconds. You may find it faster and easier than scaling.

TIP NO. 99

How to Fillet a Fish

Filleting is easy when you follow these simple steps:
- Make the first cut behind the gills. Slice down to the bone, then, without removing the blade, turn it and slice straight along the backbone to the tail.

- Note that the fillet in the diagram has been cut away from the rest of the fish. After slicing the fillet off at the tail, turn the fish over and repeat the same procedure on the other side.

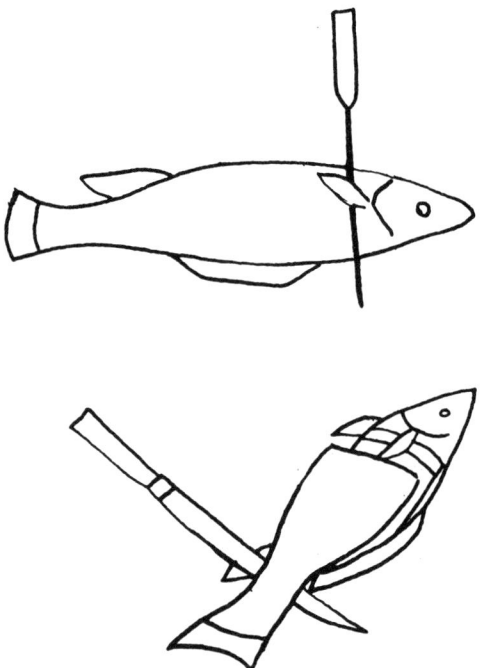

- With both sides removed, you have cut away both fillets without disturbing the fish's entrails. This is the neatest way to prepare your fish and the fastest.
- To finish the fillets, you must next remove the rib section. Again, a sharp, flexible knife is important here to avoid wasting meat. Insert the blade close to the rib bones and slice the entire section away. This should be done before the skin is removed to keep waste to a minimum.
- Remove the skin from each fillet by simply inserting the knife at the tail and "cutting" the meat from the skin. Start cutting half an inch from the tail end of skin, allowing a wedge for the best grip.

- Each fillet is now ready for pan or freezer. Note that there is no waste. Remember not to overwash the fillets. This will preserve the tasty juices and keep the meat in its firm natural state.
- Cutting out the cheeks is the next important step. Few fishermen know that the cheeks are the filet mignon of the

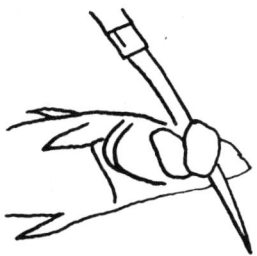

fish. Although small, they are tasty and well worth saving. The cheek fillets of walleye are a treat indeed.
- Slice into the cheek where indicated, and then scoop out the meat with the blade, peeling away the skin. Repeat the same procedure on the other side. Many fishermen save these cheeks until they have accumulated enough for a whole meal.

- You should wind up with the fish head, entrails, spine, fins, and tail intact. This is the neatest way to prepare most game fish, and, once you've mastered it, also the easiest.

TIP NO. 100

How to Pickle Fish

All of us catch fish that for one reason or another are not worth cooking. They may be too small, too bony, too oily, or have a muddy flavour. Carp and sheepshead taste coarse and muddy. Yellow perch or bullheads from farm ponds may be stunted. Or, perhaps you have caught some bony fish such as chain pickerel and suckers or some oily eels.

Pickle them. If you like rollmops made of pickled herring, you would like pickled fish of all of the species mentioned above.

Pickling is one of the oldest methods of preserving food. It is easy. Vinegar is the basic pickling ingredient. The acid in the vinegar works to soften the flesh and dissolve the bones. Herbs, spices, and onions are added to the vinegar to give the fish a distinctive flavor.

Here's how to pickle a batch of fish: The larger fish are best filleted, the smaller should be scaled or skinned, gutted, and the head, tail, and fins removed. Cut away the thin belly skin. Cut the fish or the fillets into bite-sized chunks. It takes about a pound of fish pieces to fill a quart jar.

Soak the fish pieces in a brine solution for twenty-four to forty-eight hours. The salt brine solution consists of two cups of salt to a gallon of water. Use only pure granular salt — non-iodized, sometimes called kosher salt. The use of non-iodized salt is important as the iodine used in iodized salt blends with the vinegar in the pickling solution to give the fish an unpleasant taste.

Use a plastic bucket or an earthenware crock; for soaking the fish in brine, do not use anything metallic.

After the fish pieces have been in the brine for the prescribed period, take them out, drain them, and rinse them in clean cold water. (The brine removes all blood from the fish pieces by osmosis.)

Now you start the actual pickling. Quart Mason jars are the best, but any large jars from instant coffee, pickles, or sauerkraut can be used. The pickling liquid is one half water and one half vinegar. Use clear, distilled vinegar labelled 5% acid. To this mixture, add a prepared pickling mixture of spices and herbs. This pickling mixture can be found on most supermarket spice shelves. Or, if you wish, use a mixture of one half teaspoon each of allspice, black pepper, white pepper, mustard seeds, and tarragon. This is ample for pickling five pounds of fish chunks. Now, dice some onions and get out a few bay leaves. If you like, you can also cut up a red pepper and separate a garlic bulb into cloves.

With sweet-fleshed fish such as perch, herring, suckers, catfish, and eels, put a layer of onions on the bottom of your pickling jar followed by a layer of fish chunks. Alternate the onions and fish all the way to the top. Somewhere in the middle, add a bay leaf, and, if you wish, a garlic clove and a piece of red pepper. When the jar is almost full, pour the pickling solution right to the top. Seal the jar, inverting and shaking it to get any trapped air out. Your fish are now pickling.

Muddy-tasting fish such as carp or sheepshead require a little different technique. After brining, take the fish pieces out and rinse them. Take your brine solution with the spices mixed in and boil it on the stove for ten minutes. Then add a half-cup of brown sugar. When the sugar has dissolved, put the fish into the hot solution and simmer for fifteen minutes. This partial cooking allows the pickling solution to penetrate the fish pieces.

After the fish have cooked for fifteen minutes, take the pot off the stove, drain off the pickling solution, and let it cool. Put the fish pieces into jars, alternating them with layers of sliced or diced onion. When the pickling liquid has cooled sufficiently, pour it on top of the fish in the jars. Again, make certain that no air is trapped in the jars.

Store in the refrigerator for about two months. By this time the fish will be well pickled and you are in for a treat.

As you gain in proficiency, try making rollmops and other fancy tidbits. Experiment with wine vinegar or cider vinegar for distinctive flavors.

Although fish pickled in this way will last a year and perhaps longer, I do not advise keeping them much longer than six months, just to be on the safe side.

I keep my pickled fish in my beer refrigerator and when fishing friends drop in, the pickled fish, washed down with beer, help swallow some of their tales.

TIP NO. 101

How to Cook a Shore Lunch

My last tip — three outstanding ways to cook your shore lunch after a good morning of fishing.

Plank Broiling

Cut off fish head, fins, and gut the fish. Cut your fish in half down the back, leaving the belly intact. Spread the fish on a plank of wood and tack it down with pegs or nails. Then butter

A shore lunch of freshly caught fish is a delightful part of any fishing trip.

and salt the meat. Place the plank near a flaming fire, but be careful not to burn it. The plank should be turned upside down occasionally to ensure even broiling. When ready, fish will flake when tested with a fork.

Foil Baking

Place fillets on a sheet of aluminum foil. Next, add a layer of potatoes cut into thin slices, plus several chunks of butter; finally add chopped onions for additional flavor. Top this with a second fillet and wrap carefully in a tight roll, folding the ends and top securely. Next, place the foil on hot coals turning over after approximately fifteen minutes. Total cooking time is about thirty minutes.

Skillet Frying

Clean the fish and wipe dry. Then flour with cornmeal, pancake, or biscuit mix. An easy way to flour fish is by shaking it in a paper or plastic sack. If egg batter and milk are used, fish should be covered with crackers or bread crumbs.

Place about a quarter of an inch of oil or butter in the skillet, preheating the skillet until it is hot but not smoking. Next, place the fish on one side and wait until it browns. Then turn over, and repeat the process on the reverse side. When the fish flakes with a fork, remove it from the skillet and drain on absorbent paper.

Acknowledgments

This book would have been much harder to put together without the assistance of a number of tackle testers, outdoor writers, and other fishing experts connected with fishing tackle manufacturers. I extend my thanks to the following for the use of their fine fishing tips. If there is anyone I have forgotten, it is accidental and I apologize.

Fred Aborgast Company, 313 West North Street, Akron, Ohio 44303:
    Tip No. 10 (by Dick Kotis)

Burke Fishing Lures, Division of McClellan Industries Incorporated, 1969 South Airport Road, Traverse City, Michigan 49684:
    Tips No. 58 and 59

Connecticut Flyfishers:
    Tip No. 27 (by Ron Zowoysky)

Cordel Tackle Company Incorporated, P.O. Box 2020, Hot Springs, Arkansas 71901:
    Tip No. 39 (by Jim Littleton)

Creek Chub Company, Garrett, Indiana 46738:
    Tip No. 49 (from "Bait-Casting Guide")

Daiwa Corporation, 14011 Normandie Avenue, Gardenia, California 90249:
    Tips No. 20, 46, and 51 (from "Fish the U.S.A. with Daiwa")

E. I. Du Pont de Nemours and Company Incorporated, Wilmington, Delaware 19898:
    Tips No. 19 and 80

Lou J. Eppinger Manufacturing Company, 6340 Schaefer Road, Dearborn, Michigan 48126:
    Tip No. 48 (from "All About Fishing with Eppinger's Famous Dardevles, 1971")

Fenwick Incorporated, P.O. Box 729, Westminster, California 92683:
    Tip No. 8 (by Jim Gilford)

Tip No. 22 (by Milt Rosco)
Tip No. 24 (by Charles Loughridge)
Tip No. 28 (by Jim Bashline)
Tip No. 60
Tip No. 62 (by Bill Resman)
Tip No. 85 (by Nick Karas)
Tip No. 89

Fisherman's Information Bureau, 20 North Worker Drive, Chicago, Illinois 60606:
Tips No. 35, 44, and 78 (from "How to Catch Fish in Fresh Water")

Johnson Reels Company, Johnson Park, Monkato, Minnesota 56001:
Tips No. 3 and 70 (from "Virgil Ward Championship Fishing Guide")

Lazy Ike Corporation, Fort Dodge, Iowa 50501:
Tips No. 2 and 17 (by Dick Goreham)
Tip No. 12 (by Tim Renkin)
Tips No. 14 and 101 (from press release "Outfitting Your Tackle Box")

Lindy/Little Joe Lures, Division of Ray-O-Vac Corporation, P.O. Box 488, Brainerd, Minnesota 56401:
Tips No. 36, 63, 65, and 88

Lowrance Electronics Manufacturing Company, 1200 East Skelly Drive, Tulsa, Oklahoma 74128:
Tips No. 74 and 82 (from "The Fun of Electronic Fishing")
Tip No. 75 (from "New Guide to Salmon and Trout Fishing" by Erwin Bauer)

Newton Line Company, Homer, New York 13077:
Tip No. 81 (from "Line Tips for Fishermen")

Normark Corporation, 1710 East 78th Street, Minneapolis, Minnesota 55423:
Tips No. 79 and 99

The Orvis Company, Manchester, Vermont 05254:
Tip No. 26 (by Dave Kashner)
Tips No. 56 and 83

Penn Fishing Tackle Manufacturing Company, 3020 West

Hunting Park Avenue, Philadelphia, Pennsylvania 19132:
    Tip No. 1 (from "Penn Helps You to Enjoy Fishing")
Scientific Anglers Incorporated, P.O. Box 2001, Midland, Michigan 48640:
    Tips No. 4 and 5 (from "To Cast a Fly")
    Tips No. 31, 32, and 34 (from "Flyfishing for Bass and Panfish")
    Tip No. 37 (from "Flyfishing Bulletin, Volume II")
Sevenstrand Tackle Manufacturing Company, P.O. Box 729, Westminster, California 92683:
    Tip No. 76
Shakespeare Company, Sporting Goods Division, 241 East Kalamazoo Avenue, Kalamazoo, Michigan 49001:
    Tip No. 84 (from "Secrets of Successful Fishing" by Henry Shakespeare)
Sheldon's Incorporated, Antigo, Wisconsin 54409:
    Tips No. 9 and 93 (from "Mepps Killers, 1972-1973 Fisherman's Guide")
Span, courtesy of Eldred (trout fishing) Preserve, Precision Valve Corporation, P.O. Box 309, Yonkers, New York 10702:
    Tip No. 23
Uncle Josh Bait Company, Fort Atkinson, Wisconsin 53538:
    Tip No. 69 (from "How and Why to Use Salmon Eggs")
Zebco, Consumer Division, Brunswick Incorporated, P.O. Box 270, Tulsa, Oklahoma 74101:
    Tip No. 57 (from "Worm Fishing for Bass" by Homer Circle)

  My thanks are also extended to the following for use of the photographs in this text:
    Alyson Knap, pages 1, 6, 13, 23, 36;
    Ontario Ministry of Industry and Tourism, pages 5, 10, 14, 16, 18, 33, 37;
    Ontario Ministry of Natural Resources, pages 12, 20;
    Gapen Fishing Tackle, page 17;
    Manitoba Government Travel, page 19.
    Line drawings for tips 41, 45, and 50 by Alyson Knap.